How To Bake Without Baking Powder

The Little Series of Homestead How-Tos
from *5 Acres & A Dream*

How To Bake Without Baking Powder

*modern and historical alternatives
for light and tasty baked goods*

Leigh Tate

Kikobian Books
www.kikobian.com

This book was built from the ground up with open source software on an open source operating system: Ubuntu Linux 12.04 (Precise Pangolin), Xfce 4.10 Desktop Environment, LibreOffice Writer 3.5.7.2 word processor, Notes 1.7.7 quick notes plugin, gedit 3.4.1 text editor, Gimp 2.8 photo editor, and Scribus desktop publisher version 1.4. Also used were open source fonts EB Garamond, EB Garamond SC, and Linux Biolinum (all SIL Open Font License Version 1.1), and Liberation Sans (GNU General Public License v.2).

ISBN: 978-0-9897111-3-5

Kikobian Books
www.kikobian.com

*This book is dedicated to everyone who desires
to preserve the traditional knowledge and
skills of the self-reliant, low-tech, simple life.*

Contents

List of Charts

Acknowledgements

I want to thank three fellow blogging homesteaders for their enthusiastic support for this project: Elizabeth Beavis of *Eight Acres*, Jake Kruger of *The Homestead Laboratory*, and Anna Hess of *The Walden Effect*. Their input, feedback, and encouragement came at just the right times and in just the right places.

Preface

When I published *5 Acres & A Dream The Book: The Challenges of Establishing a Self-Sufficient Homestead*, I described it as neither a how-to nor a why-to book. Although it contains quite a bit of practical advice about many homesteading skills, it is mostly the story of our journey toward simpler, sustainable, more self-reliant living. *The Little Series of Homestead How-Tos* is a complement to that book. It is a work in progress which will eventually include all of the skills mentioned in *5 Acres & A Dream The Book* and *Critter Tales*, plus other how-tos as well. I hope they will encourage you, my readers, toward your own self-reliant lifestyles.

How This Little Book Came To Be

My interest in the topic of baking without baking powder stems from my lifestyle goal of sustainable living and increased self-reliance. It's a satisfying feeling to do more for myself and to rely less on having to buy everything.

When my husband and I began our homesteading journey, however, we brought with us the ways we were used to doing things. We have gradually realized that our modern culture's means and methods often don't fit our goals as homesteaders. Because of that, we have turned more and more to traditional agrarian skills, learning how to make our own, make do, and buy less.

The Little Series of Homestead How-Tos stems from a desire to share what we're learning. This particular volume came about because I am continually exploring the limitations of our self-reliance. I find myself asking, "What would I do if I couldn't buy, trade, or barter for it?" In this case, what would I do if I couldn't get baking powder?

My research into baking powder and it's alternatives has been fascinating to me. It's introduced me to the science of baking and kitchen chemistry, plus led to some fun experimentation. In sharing all of that, the reading may be a bit technical at times, but I hope you find it as interesting as I do.

What Is Baking Powder?

Baking powder is the primary leavening agent used to make baked goods rise. When all the ingredients are mixed into a batter, the baking powder plus liquid cause a chemical reaction which results in the familiar light texture we enjoy in muffins, cakes, biscuits, waffles, and other baked goods. How does it work? Baking powder contains baking soda, an alkaline substance, an acidic ingredient such as cream of tartar, and a buffer such as corn starch. When the powder combines with the liquid in the recipe, the acid and alkali react chemically and bubble out as carbon dioxide. The buffer increases shelf life by absorbing moisture. It delays the chemical reaction which would neutralize the baking powder.

There are two kinds of baking powder: single-acting and double-acting.

Single-acting baking powders contain baking soda and one acid.

Tartrate Baking Powders contain tartaric acid (cream of tartar). Cream of tartar is fast-acting when liquid is added, so baking must follow mixing quickly.

Phosphate Baking Powders contain a phosphate such as calcium acid phosphate, sodium aluminum phosphate, or disodium pyrophosphate. These also react with liquid to create carbon dioxide but more slowly than tartrate baking powders.

SAS Baking Powders contain sodium aluminum sulfate. Its chemical reaction is triggered by heat rather than liquid, so most of the rising occurs in the oven. It is considered a slow-acting baking powder. However, it can impart a bitter taste to the final product, so small quantities are best.

Kosher for Passover Baking Powders are single-acting and contain potato starch rather than corn starch.

Double-acting baking powders contain a base and two acids, usually SAS plus tartaric acid and one of the phosphates. These chemicals react at slightly different times: one when liquid is added to the batter, the other when baking temperatures are hot enough. The advantage to this is that it allows a 15 to 20 minute delay before the leavening power is dissipated from the batter. Double-acting is the most common baking powder on the consumer market today, and is usually the one called for in most recipes.

Typical proportions are 1 to 1½ teaspoons of baking powder per cup of flour. A heavier batter, i.e. containing whole grain flours, seeds, nuts, raisins, chocolate chips, etc., will require more baking powder than a plain flour batter.

You can also make your own.

Homemade Baking Powder

1 part baking soda
2 parts cream of tartar
1 part corn starch or arrowroot powder

Mix thoroughly and store in an airtight container. In recipes, use the same amount of homemade baking powder as store-bought.

Keep in mind that all baking powder has a shelf life, usually said to be six to twelve months, depending on the amount of humidity to which it is exposed. You can check this if you wish.

To Test the Potency of Baking Powder

Add	_To_
1 tsp baking powder	⅓ C hot water

Results: it should bubble vigorously.

Discard the baking powder if it doesn't react when tested.

Alternatively, keep baking soda and cream of tartar on hand as individual ingredients, and add them when mixing the batter.

To Substitute Cream of Tartar & Baking Soda for Baking Powder:
For each teaspoon of baking powder use:
½ tsp Cream of Tartar   _and_   ¼ tsp Baking Soda

The remaining ¼ teaspoon in baking powder is starch and is not necessary for the chemical reaction. Unlike double-acting baking powder, however, this combination has a quick reaction time. For best results, bake immediately.

Is it possible to make light, tender baked goods without baking powder? Yes! This little book will introduce you to a number of ways to leaven baked goods without baking powder.

Baking Soda (The Alkali)

Once known as saleratus, baking soda has been around for a long time. Today, it is sodium bicarbonate (bicarbonate of soda), and has many household uses: toothpaste, facial scrub, deodorizer, cleaning agent, treatment for insect bites, to decrease the cooking time for dried beans, etc. It has a pH of 8.4. In baking, it is usually combined with something acidic, such as cream of tartar or buttermilk. Once liquid is added to the batter, a chemical reaction releases carbon dioxide bubbles which causes the dough or batter to rise.

In some cookie and cracker recipes, baking soda is the only leavening agent listed in the ingredients. This is because sodium bicarbonate undergoes thermal decomposition if baking temperatures are hot enough. When the internal temperature of the cookie reaches 248°F (120°C) or higher, sodium bicarbonate releases carbon dioxide and water. This works best with thin crispy products such as cookies and crackers, rather than cakes and muffins.

Because it is commonly available, baking soda is a good staple to keep on hand for leavening quick breads, but I'll discuss a few historical alternatives later in the book.

In the recipe section you will find two recipes which use baking soda exclusively as their leavening agent:

Butter Crackers, page 57.
Scottish Oat Crackers, page 58.

Cream of Tartar
(The Acid)

Cream of tartar is another item commonly found in the kitchen pantry. Other names for it are tartaric acid, potassium bitartrate, potassium hydrogen tartrate, potassium acid tartrate, or monopotassium tartrate. It is a byproduct of wine making, formed during the fermentation of grapes. It is acidic with a pH of 5 and is the acid in tartrate baking powder.

Common kitchen uses include combining with baking soda for leavening, to stabilize egg whites in meringues, to keep color in simmered vegetables, as an ingredient in homemade play dough, and for a creamy texture in icings, frostings, and fudge, because it helps prevent sugar from crystallizing.

Cream of tartar is also well-known as a natural cleaning agent: mixed with vinegar or lemon juice to remove stains, mixed with hydrogen peroxide to remove rust, or mixed with water to clean stains from porcelain. Home dyers use it to assist the mordanting process in natural dying.

For leavening baked goods use two parts cream of tartar to one part baking soda. (See chart on the bottom of page 2.)

No cream of tartar? There are numerous common substitutes. We'll take a look at those in the next chapter.

Recipes using cream of tartar with baking soda:
1800's Soda Biscuit, page 39.
Crisp Cookies, page 52.
Soda Crackers, page 57.

Common Kitchen Substitutes for Cream of Tartar

Old-time baking recipes often call for baking soda and sour milk or buttermilk. Thanks to pasteurization, sour milk is a thing of the past, and although cultured buttermilk is easy to find at the grocery store it doesn't usually make its way onto many shopping lists. Commonly recommended substitutes are:

Vinegar
Lemon juice
Molasses (treacle)
Yogurt
Cocoa powder (natural or non-processed, not Dutch cocoa)

The acidity of each of these items varies, so the substitution for cream of tartar is not a straight teaspoon for teaspoon. The other consideration is that most of them are liquids, so adjustments sometimes need to be made with other liquids in the recipe.

Obviously, some these ingredients will change the flavor of the final product. This is one reason for the preference for cream of tartar with baking soda. Depending on the recipe, however, they may be perfectly suited to the desired result, for example, natural cocoa in chocolate cake or molasses in gingerbread.

Proportions? The following are commonly recommended.

Common Kitchen Substitutes for Cream of Tartar		
For each teaspoon of baking powder substitute:		
Kitchen Acid	**Amount**	**Baking Soda**
Vinegar	½ tsp	¼ tsp
Lemon juice	½ tsp	¼ tsp
Molasses (treacle)	⅜ C	¼ tsp
Cocoa powder (natural)	¼ C	¼ tsp
Yogurt	½ C	½ tsp

Recipes?

Vinegar and baking soda:
   Vegan Chocolate Cake, page 51.
   Wacky Cake, page 52.
   White House Ginger Cookies, page 56.
Molasses and baking soda:
   Gramma Wilson's Ginger Cookies, page 53.
   White House Ginger Snaps, page 56.
Yogurt and baking soda:
   Ricotta Biscuits, page 38.
   Ginger Fig Cake, page 45.

Also see:
   "How To Make Sour Milk," page 7.
   "How To Make Cultured Buttermilk," page 9.
   "Cocoa Powder: Natural Versus Dutch," page 10.

How To Make Sour Milk

Although sour milk was once fairly common it is rarely found today unless one keeps their own cow or goats. Since it is called for in many old recipes, substitutions for it are commonly offered: mix one tablespoon of vinegar or lemon juice in one cup of milk and let stand for about five minutes. Now that you understand the principles of leavening, however, you know that you can simply add the lemon juice or vinegar and milk to the batter at the same time. You'll get the same leavening power without the wait, and the tasters of your final baked goods will be none the wiser. If you'd like to try authentic sour milk, however, and have access to fresh milk right out of the cow or goat, here's how to make it.

The souring of milk happens as the naturally occurring lactobacillus in the milk turn the lactose (milk sugar) into lactic acid. As they multiply the milk becomes increasingly acidic (sour). This is the same process that occurs in lacto-fermenting cabbage to make sauerkraut. Pasteurization kills all bacteria including lactobacillus. This is why raw milk sours and pasteurized milk putrefies.

NOTE: The following directions will only work with raw milk! This will not work with pasteurized milk! As a precaution, only use raw milk from a source that uses sanitary methods for milking and cleaning equipment, and proper refrigeration for quickly cooling the milk.

The simplest way to sour milk is to leave a lidded jar of raw milk at room temperature (68-72°F/20-22°C). After about three or four days it will have a pleasant sour smell. Store in the refrigerator for up to two weeks. It will sour faster in warmer temperatures than cool.

Sample recipes using sour milk and baking soda:

Minute Biscuit, page 38.

Swedish Christmas Cookies, page 55.

Sour Milk Soda Crackers, page 58.

Buttermilk: Cultured Versus Traditional

Not all buttermilk is equal. Once a byproduct of the butter churning process, the buttermilk sold commercially is not the same stuff. Commercial buttermilk is actually an inoculated cultured milk product that has nothing to do with making butter. It is referred to as cultured buttermilk, and it is the buttermilk that most modern recipes call for.

Traditional (or natural) buttermilk is the liquid leftover from churning butter. Agitation of cream causes the fat particles to clump together as butter. The remaining liquid does not resemble the buttermilk from the grocery store: it is thin and unless the cream was cultured for cultured butter, will be somewhat sweet. It is not naturally thick and tart.

Plain, unsweetened yogurt is commonly recommended as a substitute for buttermilk in recipes. A quick substitute can be made by adding one tablespoon of lemon juice or vinegar to one cup of milk and letting it stand for about five minutes.

To make your own cultured buttermilk, however, read on.

How To Make Cultured Buttermilk

There are three ways to make cultured buttermilk: with starter, using store-bought buttermilk, or from scratch.

Method #1. One way to make buttermilk is to purchase buttermilk starter from your favorite cheese making supplier (or see "Resources" page 68). Follow the directions on the package.

Method #2 uses store-bought (already cultured) buttermilk. You will need:
   1 cup cultured buttermilk
   3 cups fresh milk (may be pasteurized)

   Mix in a quart jar and secure the lid. Let sit at room temperature (72°F/22°C) until thickened, about 24 hours. It will be thick enough to coat the glass. Store in the refrigerator.

Method #3 is to make buttermilk from scratch. You will need fresh raw milk for this method.
   Place 1 cup of filtered raw milk in a pint jar. Cover and allow it to sit for several days at room temperature until it has thickened (clabbered).
   Take ¼ cup of the clabbered milk, mix it with 1 cup of fresh milk, cover and shake well. Allow to sit at room temperature until it has clabbered. Initially this may take several days, but gradually it will take a shorter amount of time.
   Repeat this process until the milk clabbers dependably in 24 hours. It will have a mildly sour smell and tart taste.
   This is your buttermilk starter. ¾ cup will culture a quart of fresh milk. Once thickened, store in the refrigerator. It can be used as a beverage or for baking and cooking, but be sure to save ¾ cup for your next batch.

   What can you do with your newly made buttermilk? Try one of these:
   Buttermilk Biscuits, page 38.
   Cracklin' Cornbread, page 40.
   Irish Soda Bread, page 41.
   Buttermilk Dumplings, page 59.

Cocoa Powder: Natural Versus Dutch

Not all cocoa powder is the same. The difference is not so much in where the cocoa beans are grown as in how they are processed. Dutch cocoa undergoes alkalinization, a process whereby it is treated with alkaline salts such as potassium carbonate or sodium carbonate. The result is a cocoa powder that is less bitter, richer in color, and dissolves in liquids. Its disadvantages are that it cannot be used with baking soda for leavening, and that 60-90% of its natural antioxidants are destroyed in the Dutching process. Recipes using Dutch cocoa will call for baking powder as leavening.

Natural cocoa has not been treated with an alkali and is acidic enough to react with baking soda. To give this a try, here are two recipes which leaven with natural cocoa powder and baking soda:

Classic Chocolate Cake, page 44.
Fudgey Brownies, page 45.

Experts do not recommend substituting one type of cocoa for the other in most recipes. This is because the leaveners (baking powder and baking soda) are determined by the type of cocoa powder being used. That doesn't mean it can't be done, however.

To Substitute Natural or Dutch Cocoa Powder		
To Substitute For	*Use*	*Plus*
3 tbsp Dutch cocoa	3 tbsp natural cocoa	⅛ tsp baking soda
3 tbsp natural cocoa	3 tbsp Dutch cocoa	⅛ tsp cream of tartar, or vinegar, or lemon juice

Not-So-Common Kitchen Substitutes for Cream of Tartar

While doing my research for this project, I found quite a few not-so-common kitchen acids that can be used with baking soda to leaven baked goods. In addition, I did some of my own experimenting. These substitutes include (but are not limited to):

Whey (from cheese making)
Brown sugar (which is white sugar + molasses)
Maple syrup
Golden syrup
Honey
Tangy fruits and fruit juices
Coffee
Wine
Pickle juice
Sourdough starter
Citric acid
Beer or ale
Sour cream
Kefir

For the adventuresome baker, substituting not-so-common kitchen acids for cream of tartar can make for interesting and fun experimentation. But how would one go about testing them? One way would be by trial and error until satisfactory results are obtained. Or, one could follow Culinart Kosher Labs' Marc Gottlieb's example for a more scientific approach. By observing the force, speed, and duration of the reaction between citric acid and baking soda (as compared to cream of tartar and baking soda), he determined that ¼ teaspoon citric acid to 1 teaspoon baking soda was equal to the task. See "Bibliography" for the internet address to his web post.

Citric acid is used in cheese making to acidify the milk and in boiling water bath canning as a substitute for lemon juice. It may or may not be an item in your own kitchen, but there are plenty of other kitchen acids with which to experiment. See the chart on page 64 for recommended amounts to use for some of them. If you'd like to start with a tested recipe, however, try one of the following:

Coffee and baking soda:
   "Coffee Cakes," page 60.
Tangy juices and baking soda:
   Cider Cake, page 44.
   Tomato Juice Crumb Cake, page 50.
   Tomato Juice Loaf Cake, page 51.
Pickle juice and baking soda:
   Savory Cheese Biscuits, page 39.
Sour Cream and baking soda:
   White Ginger Biscuits (cookies), page 55.
   Swedish Thin Bread, page 59.

For those who are interested in the science of leavening and would like to experiment on their own, I've included a pH chart of common foods in the appendices on page 66.

Also see "How To Make Sourdough Starter," page 13.

How To Make Sourdough Starter

Sourdough starter and sourdough baking are usually discussed within the realm of yeast bread baking, because naturally occurring airborne yeasts inoculate the starter and cause the dough to rise. Lactic acid producing bacteria are also present in the starter and make it sour. If you keep sourdough starter anyway, it can be used as the acid with baking soda for leavening quick breads.

There are two ways to make a sourdough starter:
1. Get a bit from a friend and start feeding it.
2. Make it from scratch.

To start from scratch you will need:
A crock or non-metallic bowl
Cheesecloth to cover
Flour* - 2 cups to start and more to feed it once it gets going
2 cups warm, non-chlorinated water (chlorine kills the natural yeasts)
¼ cup whey (optional, but I find it kick starts the starter)

NOTE: Some sourdough starter recipes call for baking yeast. This will somewhat guarantee the results, but you can try it without if you wish.
*Rye flour is the most recommended, but any will do, even white flour.

Mix the flour and water in the crock. It will be soupy. Cover with cheesecloth. This will allow airborne yeasts in, but keep out insects like fruit flies. Let the crock sit on the countertop at room temperature and stir daily.

After a couple of days it will begin to bubble. This is the yeast working. Add about a quarter cup of flour daily for the next several days to feed the starter. Make sure you stir in the flour well. Add more warm water if the starter seems too thick.

After about a week or so, the starter is ready to use. Remember to save some for a new batch.

To feed it: It must be fed every few days with more flour, leftover dough or batter, or leftover cooked cereal. To take a break from sourdough baking, store the starter in an airtight container in the fridge or freezer.

The only other consideration in using sousrdough starter as a quick bread leavener is the consistency of the starter. Since sourdough starter can be thick or thin (thicker contains more yeast), add milk or water to the batter as needed for the right consistency.

To Substitute Sourdough Starter for Baking Powder	
Replace	_With_
1 C of liquid in recipe	1 C thin sourdough starter _and_
and the baking powder	baking soda (same amount as the baking powder)

Here are a few recipes which use sourdough starter and baking soda to leaven, no rising time required:

Herman Friendship Cake, page 46.
Sourdough Carob Chip Cake, page 49.
Sourdough Zucchini Muffins, page 60.
Sourdough Blueberry Pancakes, page 61.

Are There Substitutes for Baking Soda?

The premise of baking without baking powder is based on a previously mentioned chemical reaction. Simplified, the reaction is:

$$an\ acid + an\ alkali = carbon\ dioxide$$

It's the carbon dioxide bubbles which cause the batter or dough to rise.

I've discussed several ways to replace baking powder in quick bread recipes, each using baking soda as the alkali with your choice of an acidic ingredient. But what about the baking soda? Is there a kitchen substitute for that?

Almost all foods are somewhat acidic with a pH lower than 7 (neutral). Baking soda is one of the few that is alkaline (pH of 8.4). Other common food-grade alkalis are milk of magnesia (pH of 10.5), pickling lime (pH of 12.4), baker's ammonia (pH of 9), and eggshells which contain calcium carbonate (pH of 9.4).

Milk of Magnesia (magnesium hydroxide) is a laxative, which definitely does not recommend it for cooking.

Pickling Lime (calcium hydroxide) is used in pickle making (to crisp pickles), to nixtamalize corn, and to make crisp Asian noodles.

Baker's Ammonia (ammonium carbonate) is the modern version of hartshorn, which is listed as an ingredient in a number of old European baking recipes.

Eggshells (containing calcium carbonate) are commonly used as a calcium source by vegetable and flower gardeners.

Could all of these be used as a substitute for baking soda? According to basic chemistry, no. Remember my premise that an acid + a base = carbon dioxide? Well, it's actually a little more technical than that. The base must be a carbonate.

$$acid + carbonate = salt + water + carbon\ dioxide$$

while

$$acid + hydroxide = salt + water.$$

Of the four food-grade alkalis mentioned above, milk of magnesia and pickling lime are hydroxides, which means they will not create carbon dioxide when reacting with an acid. Baker's ammonia is a carbonate which has been used historically in baking. We'll take a look at that in the next chapter.

Of eggshells, Jake at *The Homestead Laboratory* blog conducted several experiments using them as a carbonate source for leavening. He experimented with various methods of extracting the calcium carbonate from eggshells for baking, tried purchased pure calcium carbonate, and also baked with powdered eggshell. While the results did not equal baking soda as a leavener, he reported a pretty fair biscuit with the following.

To Substitute Eggshell for Baking Soda	
For	*Use*
1 tsp baking soda	4 tsp powdered eggshell

Web address for Jake's blog posts can be found in the bibliography on pages 75 and 76.

Baker's Ammonia (Hartshorn)

A hart is a male deer. The horn is the antler. Traditional hartshorn is just what the name implies—the powdered antler of male deer. It was once a common ingredient, and is frequently found in old German and Scandinavian cookie recipes.

The modern version is called "baker's ammonia" (ammonium carbonate). Not to be confused with household ammonia (ammonium hydroxide), it is activated by heat rather than moisture. Its best use is in small crisp cookies, which allow the ammonia gases to escape during baking, such as Lebkuchen and Springerle. It is said to give a lightness and fluffiness to the cookies that baking soda and baking powder do not. It does impart an ammonia flavor to raw cookie dough and the cookies do smell of ammonia while baking, but it is preferred for certain types of cookies because it leaves no bitter or alkaline aftertaste, and the cookies store well.

Recipes commonly call to dissolve the hartshorn in liquid before adding to the dough.

Most people don't keep baker's ammonia around, but in traditional hartshorn recipes baking powder or baking soda can be used in its place.

**To Substitute Baker's Ammonia
for Baking Powder or Baking Soda**

For	_Use_
1 tsp baking powder _or_ 1¼ tsp baking soda	1 tsp baker's ammonia

---

Side notes of interest:

Hartshorn was used as gelatin from about the 1600s to the mid-1800s.

Smelling salts are made of ammonium carbonate.

It will evaporate if not stored in a tightly sealed container.

The following recipes use baker's ammonia as the primary leavening agent:

German Christmas Cookies, page 53.

Springerle, page 54.

Swedish Christmas Crackers, page 58.

Before There Was Baking Soda: Potash, Pearlash, & Saleratus

The historical precursors of baking soda were derived from hardwood ashes. The very first patent awarded in the United States was in 1790 for an apparatus and process to make potash and pearlash from those ashes. It is the potassium carbonate in the ashes which provides the leavening action, so making potash was the first step in refining ashes for a consistent product.

Potash is simple enough to make for a home science experiment. Hardwood ashes are stirred into hot water in a glass, plastic, or ceramic container. After the ashes have settled, the floating chunks of charcoal are removed and the liquid is carefully poured off. It is boiled until only a whitish powder remains. (See "Resources" for where to find step-by-step instructions.) The result is potash. It is a mixture of various potassium salts, including potassium carbonate. In addition to cooking, potash was historically used for bleaching textiles, making glass, and making soft soap. Even so, pearlash was preferred at that time for baking.

Pearlash is pure potassium carbonate, made by burning off the impurities of potash in a kiln. It was more consistent in results, not to mention more aesthetic with it's pearly-white color.

Saleratus (potassium bicarbonate) was originally made from pearlash (potassium carbonate). Then chemists discovered that by exposing pearlash to carbon dioxide a more potent leavener could be created. The name "saleratus" was taken from the Latin for "aerated salt."

In the mid-1800s sodium bicarbonate was developed in Europe and found to be superior to potassium bicarbonate. The first American manufacturers of sodium bicarbonate called their product "saleratus," but later it became known as baking soda.

I'm not the only one with an interest in these historical leaveners. While doing online research for this book, I found a few brave souls who had experimented with those early leaveners. (See "Bibliography" for the internet addresses to all.) Their results were highly variable.

Revolutionary War reenactor David Manthey compared biscuits made with seven different leaveners: baking soda, baking powder, baker's ammonia, potassium bicarbonate, home-made potash, active dry yeast, and sourdough starter. This particular experiment ranked the two batches made with home-made potash (one with vinegar and one without) to be equivalent to an unleavened sample.

Professional baker and living historian Jeff Pavlik compared batches of muffins baked with plain water, barm (a brewing byproduct, see "Other Historical Leaveners," page 28), baking soda, and pearlash with either water or ale (both carbonated and non-carbonated). It was interesting to note how the carbonated ale assisted the rise with both pearlash and baking soda.

Sarah Lohman at the *Four Pound Flour* blog tried a historical pearlash cookie recipe but with disappointing results. She reported that the bitter, astringent aftertaste made them uneatable. The interesting conversation which follows in the comments suggests that her copy of the recipe called for too much pearlash and that more acid was needed. This corresponded to a statement I found at the *German Baking Glossary* website:

> "When dissolved in water, pearlash decomposes to potassium and carbonate ions; the carbonate becomes carbonic acid, which bubbles out as carbon dioxide. The potassium recombines with the water's hydroxide ions to produce potassium hydroxide (KOH), which is also alkaline. In order to prevent it giving a bitter or soapy taste to the food, you have to add an acid to neutralize the potassium hydroxide, but you can get all of the leavening power without acidic ingredients."

At that same website, German food expert Jennifer McGavin recommends

To Substitute Potash or Pearlash for Baking Soda	
For	*Use*
½ tsp of baking soda	1 tsp of potash or pearlash

That potash requires specific proportions in a recipe was known at the time it was in common use. According to an article entitled "American Pot-Ash Cake" in the December 1799 issue of *The Scots Magazine*:

> "Please to caution those, Sir, who make this kind of cake, that they do not, in their eagerness to have it light, add pot-ash too much over the common rule, which would not only give the cake an alkaline taste, but make it as heavy as it would have been had pot-ash not entered the mixture... This is an error which experienced hands seldom commit."

For those interested in trying their hand with these historical leaveners I offer the following recipes:

Pearlash:
 Molasses Gingerbread, page 48.
 Short Cake, page 49.
 Flat-jacks, page 61.
Potash:
 American Potash Cakes, page 37.
 A Cheaper Cake, page 43.
 Handy Cake, page 46.
Saleratus:
 Indian Cake, page 41.
 Sponge Drops, page 50.

See "Resources" (page 68) for where to purchase pearlash or saleratus or for the internet address to instructions for making your own potash.

Hardwood Ashes

While my research into the historical precursors of baking soda was interesting, I wasn't sure that I wanted to try making potash myself, nor in purchasing pearlash or potassium bicarbonate with which to experiment. I wasn't interested in getting complicated, and if I wanted to stock up on anything for a hard times situation, it might as well be easy-to-come-by baking soda. However, I happened upon several statements which piqued my curiosity:

"In times past, when chemically manufactured baking soda was not available, 'ash water' was used instead. Ashes from hardwood trees contain carbonates and bicarbonate salts, which can be extracted with water. This approach became obsolete with the availability of purified baking soda." Source: *Wikipedia*, "Baking Powder."

"American women were routinely using this chemical (made at home of wood ash) in their baking." Source: *Martha Washington's Booke of Cookery and Booke of Sweetmeats.*

"It was Native Americans who first invented chemical leavening, using ashes as they did to "lighten" grain cakes." Source: *Joe Pastry*, "Where Does Irish Soda Bread Come From?"

Hardwood ashes for cooking have been common in various cultural cuisines throughout the ages: in Mexico for nixtamalization of corn for masa, in the Philippines as Lihiya, in Nigerian cuisine as Kaun or Akaun, for Scandinavian lutefisk, for making olives in the Mediterranean, in old European recipes for Greek and Polish cookies, as Pottasche in German gingerbread, browning pretzels and lye rolls, in Chinese Century eggs and Asian noodles, and in Hopi piki bread. Native Americans used wood ash to make hominy from corn. Cooking with ash is also considered a trendy gourmet technique, and think of ash-coated cheeses. Or how about paleo recipes for steaks cooked on a coal bed?

All of that might not convince you, but the prepper in me is always running in the background asking, "How would I do that if I couldn't buy or barter for it?" In this case, "How would I bake quick breads if I couldn't get baking soda? Could I somehow use hardwood ashes if I had to?" I decided to experiment.

Experiments in Baking with Wood Ash

Hardwood ashes contain carbonates similar to the ones used in modern baking powders. The problem is that the chemical composition of hardwood ash is highly variable and depends on tree type and burning temperature. This means that results could be highly unpredictable—not a good quality in a recipe. Still, for a little kitchen chemistry experiment, I figured I'd just have a go and see what happened.

Making the Ash Water

For this experiment, I collected oak and pecan ashes from our wood stove and made three solutions in different strengths: one with one tablespoon of wood ash, one with two, and the last with three tablespoons. These were stirred into ¼ cup filtered tap water and allowed to sit until the insoluble components sank to the bottom. I poured off the clear ash water through a filter to collect the soluble carbonates that I wanted.

Testing the Ash Water

My first test was for pH. Litmus paper indicated that the solutions were progressively more alkaline, with pHs of approximately 10, 11, and 12. My second test was to see how each solution would react with an acid, for which I used white vinegar. If baking soda is added to vinegar, the reaction is an immediate impressive show of vigorous bubbling. Add a little red food coloring and paper mache volcano, and you've got a school science fair project.

To my surprise, none of my ash water solutions reacted with the vinegar. When I added one tablespoon of dry wood ash to vinegar, however, I got bubbling; not as impressive as baking soda and vinegar, but it was a fair reaction nonetheless.

When my results were not what I expected I felt like I was at a crossroads. I could continue researching the chemistry of the process, or I could get on with my baking experiments. I opted to do some baking.

1st Baking Experiments with Ash Water

For my first set of baking experiments I made four batches of drop biscuits. I used one of my standard biscuit recipes but quartered the amounts.

My base recipe for the experimental biscuits was:

½ cup white flour
⅛ tsp salt
⅛ cup (2 tbsp) palm shortening
¼ cup (4 tbsp) fresh milk (not soured)
½ tsp white vinegar
¼ tsp baking soda

Baking soda was used only in the control batch. In two of the batches I replaced the baking soda with a 1:1 solution of ash water (equal parts hardwood ashes and water), but this time I used hot water because I learned that it extracts the maximum amount of potassium carbonate. I adjusted the amount of milk to keep the total liquid the same for all batches. In the last batch I substituted dry sifted wood ashes for the baking soda. Biscuits were baked at 425°F (218°C) for 8-10 minutes. The following photos show my results.

#1: control batch used baking soda and vinegar.
#2: replaced half the milk in the recipe with ash water.
#3: replaced all of the milk in the recipe with ash water
#4: used dry wood ash at twice the amount of baking soda called for

From the left: batch #1, batch #2, batch #3, and batch #4.

Experiments in Baking with Wood Ash

From the left: batch #1, batch #2, batch #3, and batch #4.

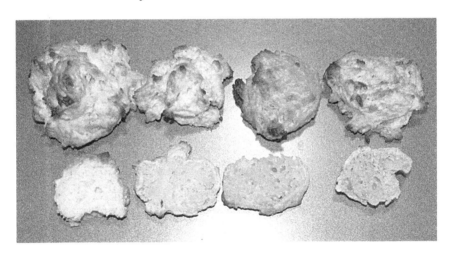

One thing I noticed immediately was that all three batches with wood ash were not completely dry inside. My conclusion was that they could have baked a little longer. Of their color, I expected the dry ash biscuit to be more grayish than it was. Even so, I didn't find the color objectionable.

How did they taste? They tasted like ordinary biscuits. No odd flavor or bitter or soapy aftertaste, which apparently is a problem when baking with pearlash (which is more concentrated because it is purified and refined). Batch #3 in which the milk was replaced with ash water had a somewhat pretzel flavor. Pretzels are dipped in lye water before baking to give them their characteristic shiny pretzel brown (known as the Maillard reaction), but apparently the lye water adds a characteristic pretzel flavor as well.

I continued to experiment with different strengths of ash water, different amounts of vinegar, and different proportions of milk. In general, I found that a very satisfactory biscuit with excellent flavor could be made with a solution of two parts water to one part hardwood ash, replacing half the milk called for in the original recipe. No, they didn't equal baking soda biscuits, but in an emergency or survival situation, or for a homeschool science experiment, they are well worth the effort.

I've not included a chart for substituting ash water for baking soda, because I haven't experimented enough to know if the proportions I used in my biscuits would be the same for other baked goods. For the daring, however, I've included two of my own ash-leavening recipes plus a traditional Native American recipe. I strongly recommend reading the next chapter before giving them a try.

Ash Water Drop Biscuits, page 37.
Survival Biscuits, page 40.
Hopi Piki Bread, page 40.

Additional notes:

1. My ash water solutions are not strong enough for soap making. (See "Ash Water Vs. Lye Water Vs. Lye Water: Are They All the Same?")
2. For leavening consistency, each batch of wood ashes should probably be tested, but as an alternative or survival method of baking, this is one for the books.

Ash Water Versus Lye Water Versus Lye Water: Are They All the Same?

Ash water is something that is often associated with old-fashioned soap making. Instructions for this abound in books and on the internet. In every case I've seen, the ash water for soap making is referred to as "lye water" or "lye."

Lye is a term which our modern minds pretty much associate with something dangerous. It's the stuff of drain cleaners and can burn one's skin. So when it comes to making one's own ash water for baking, the idea that it is also called "lye water" can be pretty scary.

There are several different chemical compounds which are referred to as "lye." One is sodium hydroxide, also called "caustic soda." This is the ingredient in oven and drain cleaners. This is the form of lye which soap makers use to make hard bar soaps. It is also used for making hominy, grits, German pretzels, black olives, Asian noodles, and to commercially wash and peel fruits and vegetables.

Potassium hydroxide is also referred to as "lye." Known as "caustic potash," it is used in the manufacture of biodiesel, as an electrolyte in alkaline batteries, and for making soft soaps. It is also sometimes found in cuticle removers and shaving creams. In food preparation, it is used as a rinse or chemical peel for fruits and vegetables. It is sometimes used as a substitute for sodium hydroxide in pretzel making, to increase shelf life of processed foods, as a thickener in ice cream, in dutching cocoa powder, and in processing soft drinks.

Hardwood ashes are composed primarily of carbonates, but also chlorides, sulfates, and hydroxides. The amounts and exact composition vary depending on the type of wood and the temperature at which it was burned.

The presence of hydroxides is the reason hardwood ash water can be used to make a soft soap, and why it is often referred to as "lye water." It isn't as strong as the pure caustic potash solution used by soap makers, however, as is evidenced by the quality of soap it produces. To obtain a stronger solution for making soap, the ash water can either be boiled down or run through a fresh batch of ashes. If the final solution can float a quarter-size portion of an egg, then it is considered strong enough to make soap.

For baking, it's the carbonates that are important, not the hydroxides, so a stronger solution is not the goal. In baking, the problem with those hydroxides is that they can impart a bitter or soapy taste to the food, just as pearlash can (see "Before Baking Soda: Potash, Pearlash, & Saleratus," page 18). The solution for this problem is to naturalize the excess alkali by increasing the acidic ingredients in the recipe. A little extra vinegar, lemon juice, or sour milk won't hurt your cake or biscuits and may help them rise better.

Common sense dictates not to splash ash water on yourself, but I can tell you from experience that it will simply feel slippery like soapy water.

Because of the general confusion about the different types of lye and lye water, I prefer to call my ash water simply that.

Other Historical Leaveners

For interest's sake and to give you all of the information I've found on the topic of baking without baking powder, I'm going to mention four more historical leaveners: barm, emptings, carbonate of soda, and corn cob soda.

Barm and emptings are yeast by-products from brewing ale, cider, and beer. Since many colonial households brewed these in the home, barm and emptings were readily available to the family baker.

Barm is the foam or froth that forms on top of the brew during fermentation. I found a number of recipes that use it, but all allow for a rising time. In other words, barm is treated as yeast. Baking with yeast is a topic all of its own, so I'll explore the use of brewing yeasts in a future how-to.

Emptings (also written as "emptins" or "emptyings") are the yeasty sediments found at the bottom of the brewing barrel. I found several recipes using emptings in quick breads, so I've included two of these in "Recipes," in case anyone does their own brewing or knows a home brewer.
A Light Cake to Bake in Small Cups, page 43.
Loaf Cake, page 48.

Carbonate of Soda is mentioned as a leavener in only one source that I have found: *Mrs. Beeton's Book of Household Management* published in 1861. A number of her baking recipes call for it. Not to be confused with bicarbonate of soda (baking soda), carbonate of soda is also referred to as sodium carbonate, soda ash, washing soda, or baked soda. Found on the laundry aisle at the grocery store, washing soda is considered a detergent booster and household cleaner. Recipes for homemade laundry soap call for it, and it it is the primary ingredient in coffee machine cleaners and automatic dishwashing powders. It is found in toothpaste and sherbet powder, and is used as a substitute for lye water for making pretzels and Asian noodles. It has a higher pH than baking soda (11.6 compared to 8.4). Most modernizations of Mrs. Beeton's recipes substitute baking soda in equal amounts.
Carbonate of soda can be made by heating baking soda to 250-300°F (125-150°C) for one hour. Store in an airtight container. You can try it in
Mrs. Beeton's Soda Bread, page 42.

Corn Cob Soda was used in the southern United States prior to and during the Civil War. Narratives from the *Federal Writers Project* describe that corn cobs were burned and the ashes saved as leavening. Although there was unanimous agreement as to the excellence of the baked goods made with corn cob soda, none of these narratives describe a detailed step-by-step process. In *The Language of the Civil War*, author John D. Wright states that red corn cobs were especially high in alkali. Ashes from these were stored in jars and water added. A teaspoon or tablespoon of this solution was used in making bread.

What About Eggs?

Eggs are another time-honored form of leavening, especially for cakes and filled pastries. The rise is not chemically induced, as it is with baking powder, but rather physically (or mechanically). Beaten eggs incorporate air into the batter which expands in the oven and causes the cake to rise. Yolks add tenderness and structural integrity to the final product and are commonly added with the other liquids. Egg whites are whipped and folded into the batter last, to maintain their structure and volume.

Tips for getting the best volume out of eggs

Temperature: Room temperature eggs are said to yield triple the volume of cold eggs. Warm eggs to room temperature by placing them in a bowl of warm water for 10 to 15 minutes.

Separate whites and yolks:

Beat separately:

Yolks until they are smooth.

Whites until they form stiff shiny peaks.

Add to the batter individually:

Yolks are added to the other liquids.

Whites are folded in last.

Bake immediately.

Choice of mixing bowl for whipping egg whites:

Copper is said to work best and stabilizes the egg whites.

Stainless steel is good if cream of tartar is used to stabilize the whites.

Aluminum imparts an unappealing grayish color to the egg whites.

Glass and plastic bowls are too slippery to obtain fluffy egg whites.

Speed: Start beating at low speed and gradually increase to medium-high. This will improve stability of the air bubbles.

Cream of Tartar: Add ⅛ teaspoon cream of tartar when the whites are in the foam stage. Sugar can be added at the soft peak stage. These help maintain stability of the beaten-in air.

Type of eggs: If you can get them, use duck eggs. In comparison to chicken eggs, duck eggs are larger and have a higher percentage of yolk. They contain more fat and protein, which means richer, fluffier, moister baked goods which rise better than those baked with chicken eggs. According to Chef Jamie Oliver, the denser albumen in duck eggs gives gluten-free baked goods better structure.

Duck eggs can be substituted one for one in recipes. Because they have a lower water content than chicken eggs, no other adjustment is necessary.

Although most recipes for cakes, cookies, and quick breads use eggs, I only listed eggs as leaveners if they either folded in whipped eggs whites, or incorporated half-a-dozen eggs or more:

Fritters, page 42.
Lady Fingers, page 47.
Philadelphia Jumbles, page 54.
Cream Puffs, page 62.

The Little Things Matter

To produce light and tasty baked goodies we want to facilitate our leavener.

Temperature Matters

Make sure the oven is properly preheated to the recommended temperature.

Heat-activated leaveners will get a better rise with room temperature ingredients.

Fats cream best at room temperature.

Fats cut-in best if chilled, but not too cold or too soft.

Eggs emulsify the batter best at room temperature.

Mixing Matters

Beating a batter, like kneading dough, develops gluten. Gluten makes bread rise but makes quick breads and cakes tough. For these, air needs to be worked in during:

Sifting of flour and dry ingredients - Lumps don't rise well.

Beating of eggs - Beat well to incorporate plenty of air.

Creaming of fat and sugar - Caster (superfine) sugar works best. As the grains cut through the fat they create tiny air bubbles which help baked goods to rise and maintain a light texture.

Baking Matters

For heat-activated chemical leaveners, such as double-acting baking powder, make sure oven temperature is correct.

For moisture-activated chemical leaveners, such as single-acting baking powder, bake immediately. Don't let the leavener lose its oomph.

Do not drop or knock cake pans to level the batter (we *want* the air bubbles).

Allow for proper heat and air circulation around your baking pans.

Convection ovens (with fans) tend to dry out baked goods, so use a conventional oven for optimal moistness.

Love Matters

When you love what you are doing, the world is a happier place. We share that happiness with others when we share the work of our hands.

Happy Baking!

Recipes

The hardest part about creating this recipe section was deciding how to organize it: by leaveners (buttermilk, vinegar, sour cream, etc)? Or by item (cakes, cookies, biscuits, etc)? Some of the recipes use only baking soda plus one acid, but many use a combination of leaveners. For example, eggs are often included in cakes, cookies, and muffins for richness and texture, not just for leavening. You will find the recipes listed in two places: at the end of the leavening agent chapters and here by recipe type.

Recipe Notes:
Vinegar and lemon juice can be substituted in the same proportions. Either white or apple cider vinegar may be used.
Sour dairy products: buttermilk, sour milk, yogurt, kefir, whey, and sour cream can be substituted in the same proportions.
Molasses, honey, maple syrup, treacle, and golden syrup can be substituted in the same proportions.
Sources of recipes are mentioned except for those found in multiple places.
Flour and fat types are given as the recipe listed them, but you can substitute these according to your personal ingredient preferences.

Biscuits

Breads

Cakes

Cookies

Crackers

Dumplings

Muffins

Pancakes

Pastry

Miscellaneous

Biscuits

American Potash Cakes

Leavening agent: potash

I found this old recipe in several sources, all dating in the very early 1800s.

> 1 *pound flour
> ¼ pound butter (½ C)
> ¼ pound sugar (2 C)
> ½ pint milk (1 C)
> 1 tsp potash
> ½ teacup cold water (6 tbsp)

Mix flour and butter. Dissolve and stir sugar into milk. Make a solution of potash in cold water. Work it into the flour to a paste of good consistence, roll out, form into cakes or biscuits. The lightness of these cakes depends greatly on the briskness of the oven.

Pound flour varies according to the kind of flour:
> 1 pound sifted white flour = 4 scant cups
> 1 pound unsifted white flour = 4 cups
> 1 pound whole wheat flour = 3½ cups

Ash Water Drop Biscuits

Leavening agents: ash water and vinegar

See "Experiments in Baking with Wood Ash," page 22.

For the ash water:
> ½ C hardwood ashes
> 1 C hot water

Slowly pour hot water over hardwood ashes. Stir and let sit for several hours or overnight until ashes have settled to the bottom of the bowl. Skim off any bits of floating wood or charcoal. Pour off the ash water through a coffee filter. The ash water will be slippery to touch.

For the biscuits:
> 2 C flour
> ½ C shortening (rendered chicken fat makes a tasty biscuit)
> ½ tsp salt
> ⅓ C ash water
> ⅓ C milk
> 2 tsp vinegar

Preheat oven to 425°F (220°C). Mix dry ingredients and cut in shortening. Combine liquids and mix into dry mixture with a fork. Drop onto ungreased baking sheet and bake about 15 minutes or until golden brown.

Alternatively, you can replace the milk and vinegar with buttermilk, sour milk, plain yogurt, kefir, or acidic whey.

Buttermilk Biscuits

Leavening agents: baking soda and buttermilk

This recipe is adapted from *The Little House Cookbook*.

    2 C unbleached flour
    1 tsp salt
    1 tsp baking soda
    ¾ C buttermilk
    3 tbsp melted lard or butter

Mix dry ingredients and work in lard or butter with hands. Mix quickly, roll out, and cut with biscuit cutter. Bake at 425°F (220°C) for 12 to 15 minutes. Serve fresh out of the oven.

Minute Biscuit

Leavening agents: sour milk and baking soda

From Marion Harland's *Common Sense in the Household: A Manual of Practical Housewifery* published in 1893.

    1 pint sour milk (2 C)
    1 tsp soda
    2 tsp melted butter
    flour to make a soft dough, just stiff enough to handle.

Mix, roll, and cut out rapidly, with as little handling as may be, and bake in a quick oven (375-400°F/190-200°C).

Ricotta Biscuits

Leavening agents: baking soda and yogurt, kefir, or whey

Fat-free biscuits born out of an abundance of homemade goats' milk ricotta.

    2 C flour
    2 tsp baking soda
    ½ tsp sea salt
    1 large egg
    1 C ricotta cheese
    ¼ C yogurt, kefir, or whey

Mix dry and wet ingredients separately, then combine mixtures and stir with a fork. Shape into biscuits and bake at 425°F (220°C) for 12 to 15 minutes or until golden brown. Serve hot.

Savory Cheese Biscuits

Leavening agents: baking soda and dill pickle juice

One of my successful experiments in baking without baking powder.

2 C flour
1½ tsp baking soda
½ tsp salt
½ C palm shortening
1 C milk (for drop biscuits - use ⅔ C milk for rolled and cut biscuits)
1 tbsp dill pickle juice
1 C shredded cheese
1½ tsp dry mustard powder
¼ tsp black pepper

Mix flour, soda, salt, mustard, and pepper. Cut shortening into flour mixture. Add milk and pickle juice and mix enough to moisten. Fold in shredded cheese and drop onto greased baking sheet. Bake at 425°F (220°C) for 10 to 12 minutes or until golden brown.

1800's Soda Biscuit

Leavening agents: baking soda and cream of tartar

From *An Army Wife's Cookbook* by Alice Kirk Grierson, circa 1880.

1 quart flour (4 C)
2 heaping tbsp lard
2 C *sweet milk
1 tsp soda
2 tsp cream of tartar
1 tsp salt

Rub soda and cream of tartar into flour dry, next the lard, lastly the milk. Work with as little handling as possible. The dough should be very soft. Cut more than half-inch thick and bake in a quick oven (375-400°F/190-200°C).

Very old recipes usually differentiate between sweet and sour milk. If using store-bought milk, sweet milk would be milk before the end of it's expiration date.

Survival Biscuits

Leavening agents: hardwood ash and vinegar

This was an experiment that turned out better than I expected. Based on color, texture, and flavor, you'd never know dry wood ashes were used in the dough.

  2 C flour
  ½ C solid fat
  ⅔ C milk or enough for proper consistency
  2 tsp vinegar
  4 tsp dry sifted hardwood ash

Mix as for ordinary biscuits and bake at 425°F (220°C) for 10 to 12 minutes or until golden brown.

Breads

Cracklin' Cornbread

Leavening agents: baking soda and buttermilk

Another of my own recipes, this one using home-churned buttermilk.

Preheat oven to 425°F (220°C). Heat a 10-inch cast iron skillet containing:
  ¼ C lard or bacon grease
Mix together dry ingredients:
  1½ C corn meal
  ½ C all-purpose flour
  1 tsp baking soda
  1 tsp salt
Mix together wet ingredients:
  1 large egg, lightly beaten
  2 C buttermilk
Stir together dry and wet and fold in:
  1 C cracklings (skimmed, cooked bits of fat and meat from fat rendering)
Pour batter into piping hot skillet. Bake until golden brown, about 25 minutes.

Hopi Piki Bread

Leavening agent: ash water

A traditional Hopi recipe.

  1 C Green Juniper or Chamisa (Rabbitbush) ash
  1 C blue cornmeal
  1 C boiling water
  3 C cold water

Mix ash with boiling water and set aside. Mix cornmeal in cold water, stir well. Slowly strain the ash water into the cornmeal. Knead until smooth. Spread thinly on hot, greased griddle. Cook until barely brown. Roll up like a jelly roll and serve.

Indian Cake

Leavening agents: saleratus and molasses

From *The American Frugal Housewife*.

    2 C Indian (corn) meal
    1 tbsp molasses
    2 C milk
    dash salt
    handful flour
    a little saleratus

Mix above into a thin batter. Pour into "a buttered bake-kettle hung over the fire uncovered, until you can bear your finger upon it, and then set down before the fire. Bake half an hour."

Irish Soda Bread

Leavening agents: baking soda and buttermilk

According to The Society for the Preservation of Irish Soda Bread, the earliest known reference to Irish Soda Bread is in the November 1836 issue of *Farmer's Magazine*. The article references an Irish newspaper in County Down. See "Bibliography" for an internet address to the society's website for more information and more recipes.

    4 C stone ground whole wheat flour
    2 C white flour
    1½ tsp baking soda
    1½ tsp salt
    2 C buttermilk

Preheat oven to 425°F (220°C). Mix together the flours, salt, and baking soda. Add the buttermilk and continue to stir until moistened, then knead in the bowl until you have a soft and slightly sticky ball. Add flour or more buttermilk as necessary to get the right consistency. Transfer dough to a lightly floured surface and roll out to a circle about 1½ inches thick. Transfer to a cast iron pan. With a sharp knife, make a cross-shaped slit in the top. Bake for 25 minutes at 425°F (220°C), then reduce the heat to 350°F (180°C) and bake for 15 minutes more. Cool on a rack at least an hour before cutting, longer is better.

Fritters

Leavening agent: eggs

From *Common Sense in the Household: A Manual of Practical Housewifery.*

> 1 pint flour (2 C)
> 4 eggs, separated
> 1 tsp salt
> 1 pint boiling water (2 C)
> *sweet lard for frying

Stir the flour into the water by degrees, and stir until it has boiled three minutes. When it is almost cold, then beat in the egg yolks, then the whites, which must be previously whipped stiff. Fry in plenty of nice sweet lard and test the heat by dropping in a teaspoonful before you risk more. If right, the batter will rise quickly to the surface in a puff-ball, spluttering and dancing, and will speedily assume a rich golden-brown. Take up as soon as done, with a skimmer, shaking it to dislodge any drops of lard that may adhere; pile in a hot dish, sift sugar over them, and send instantly to the table.

Sweet lard - I couldn't find a definition for this, so I assume it means fresh leaf lard, which is the finest, mildest grade of lard rendered from fat around the pig kidneys. Lard has a high smoking point which makes it excellent for frying.

Mrs. Beeton's Soda Bread

Leavening agents: carbonate of soda and cream of tartar

From *Mrs. Beeton's Book of Household Management.*

> To every 2 pounds (8 C) of flour allow:
> > 1 tsp of tartaric acid (cream of tartar)
> > 1 tsp of salt
> > 1 tsp of *carbonate of soda
> > 2 †breakfast-cupfuls of cold milk (1½ - 2 C)

Let the tartaric acid and salt be reduced to the finest possible powder; then mix them well with the flour. Dissolve the soda in the milk, and pour it several times from one basin to another, before adding it to the flour. Work the whole quickly into a light dough, divide it into 2 loaves, and put them into a well-heated oven immediately, and bake for an hour. Sour milk or buttermilk may be used, but then a little less acid will be needed.

Carbonate of soda - See "Other Historical Leaveners" on page 28.
†*Breakfast-cupfuls - Apparently there were different sizes of breakfast cups measuring between ¾ and 1 cup The two cupfuls called for here would be 1½ to 2 cups. The baker will have to be guided by the consistency of the dough.*

Cakes

A Cheaper Cake

Leavening agents: sour milk, molasses, and potash or pearlash

"Cheaper" is in reference to Handy Cake (page 46) with which this recipe was paired in *The Scots Magazine*.

2 pounds rye flour (7½ C)
½ pound lard (1 C)
½ pound molasses or treacle (1 C)
1 pint sour or coagulated milk (2 C)
heaped tsp of salt of tartar, potash, or pearlash dissolved in a little water

Mix and bake as for Handy Cake ("Mix ingredients and knead well. The success of this cake will depend on a sufficiency of hot coals for baking.")

The article goes on to state that the success of these cakes also depends on the correct proportion of potash to the other ingredients. Too much potash results in a heavy, alkaline-tasting cake.

A Light Cake to Bake in Small Cups

Leavening agent: emptings

This very old recipe comes from one of American's earliest cookbooks, *American Cookery* by Amelia Simmons, an American Orphan. I'm afraid what's here is all the instructions she gave us.

Half a pound sugar (1 C)
half a pound butter (1 C) rubbed into
two pounds flour (8 C)
one *glass wine
one †do. rose water
two do. emptins
‡a nutmeg (one whole nutmeg)
cinnamon
currants

One glass. I could find no information as to what this measurement might be, so it obviously depends upon one's glass!
†do. = ditto
Rose water was once a popular flavoring for baked goods.
‡ *Nutmegs were once sold as whole nuts and hand-grated by the baker with a nutmeg grater.*

Cider Cake

Leavening agents: baking soda and apple cider

Cider cake is an example of using a tangy fruit juice with baking soda for leavening. It must have been popular at one time, because there are quite a few recipe variations for it. This one comes from *Dr. Chase's Receipt Book*, published in 1887.

1½ C sugar
¾ C butter, room temperature
1⅓ C *sweet apple cider, room temperature
1 tsp baking soda
1 tsp each cinnamon and cloves
4½ C flour

Cream together the sugar and butter. Add the cider, and beat until it's all the same consistency. Add the soda and spices, followed by the flour. Bake at 350°F (180°C) for 35 to 40 minutes.

Sweet cider would be fresh, not fermented. Hard cider would be fermented.

Classic Chocolate Cake

Leavening Agents: baking soda and cocoa powder

A favorite amongst chocolate cake lovers.

⅔ C butter, softened
1⅔ C sugar
3 eggs
2 C flour
⅔ C *natural cocoa powder
1¼ tsp baking soda
1 tsp salt
1⅓ C milk

Cream butter and sugar until fluffy. Add eggs, one at a time, beating well after each addition. Combine flour, cocoa, baking soda and salt; add to creamed mixture alternately with milk, beating until smooth after each addition. Pour batter into a greased and floured 13x9-inch pan. Bake at 350°F (180°C) for 35 to 40 minutes or until cake tests done. Frost with your favorite frosting.

See "Cocoa Powder: Natural Versus Dutch" page 10.

Fudgey Brownies

Leavening agents: baking soda, cocoa powder, and coffee

A family favorite.

    1⅓ C flour
    1 tsp baking soda
    ½ tsp salt
    ¾ C natural cocoa powder
    2 tbsp coffee
    2 eggs
    1 tsp vanilla extract
    1⅔ C sugar
    ¾ C butter, melted

Mix dry ingredients and set aside. Cream sugar and butter, add eggs, coffee, and vanilla. Stir in dry ingredients just until mixed. Batter will be very thick. Spread in a greased 9x13-inch cake pan and bake 15 to 20 minutes at 350°F (180°C). Brownie edges will be pulling from sides of pan but it will still leave a finger imprint in the center. Do not overbake. Not sure how many it makes because they never last long enough to count.

Ginger Fig Cake

Leavening agents: baking soda, plain yogurt, and egg whites

Another of my own recipes. I use plain yogurt in this recipe, but any sour dairy would do.

    2 C unbleached flour
    1½ C unbleached sugar
    1 tsp baking soda
    1 tsp sea salt
    1 tsp ground ginger
    ½ C palm shortening
    1 C plain yogurt
    1 tsp vanilla
    3 egg whites, beaten stiff
    1 C mashed figs (fresh, re-hydrated dried, or drained frozen or canned)

Cream sugar and shortening. Add remaining ingredients except egg whites and mix well. Fold in egg whites and pour into greased bundt pan. Bake for about 40 to 45 minutes at 350°F (180°C) or until done.

Handy Cake

Leavening agents: sour milk and potash or pearlash

From *The Scots Magazine*, dated December 1799, which states that the recipe makes a "fine and spongy cake." From the instructions, however, I'm guessing this makes a much heavier cake than we moderns are used to. Also see "A Cheaper Cake," page 43.

    2 pounds of good wheaten flour (3½ C whole wheat flour)
    ½ pound butter (1 C)
    ½ pound sugar stirred in (1 C)
    1 pint sour or coagulated milk (2 C)
    heaped tsp of salt of tartar, potash, or pearlash dissolved in a little water

Mix ingredients and knead well. The success of this cake will depend on a "sufficiency of hot coals" for baking.

Herman Friendship Cake

Leavening agents: baking soda and sourdough starter

I debated whether or not to include this recipe because the starter calls for yeast (which sourdough starters often do, see page 13.) Anyway, it's the starter with baking soda as leavener that's the point, so I included it for your consideration.

This recipe is from a newspaper clipping which must be at least 30 years old. I used to give a cake plus a cup of Herman starter as gifts to friends or new neighbors.

Herman Starter
    1 package dry yeast
    ½ C warm (105°F/40°C) water
    2 tsp sugar or honey
    2½ C all-purpose flour
    2 C additional warm water

Mix yeast, ½ cup warm water, and sugar or honey. When yeast is foamy, stir in flour and additional water. Place in a large crock or glass jar. Do not use a metal container. Cover with damp cloth and rubber band. Keep at room temperature for five days, stirring daily with a wooden spoon.

Day 5 - feed Herman 1 cup flour, 1 cup milk, and ¾ cup sugar. Keep covered with damp towel at room temperature. Stir daily.

Day 10 - feed Herman again: 1 cup flour, 1 cup milk, ¾ cup sugar. Stir.

Herman is now ready to be divided up and baked. Use two cups for baking. Save one cup and continue feeding. On the 5th and 10th days for 10 more days (when Herman will be ready to bake again) give two cups to friends to grow.

Herman Friendship Cake
  2 C Herman starter
  2 C flour
  3 eggs
  ⅔ C light salad oil
  ½ tsp salt
  2 tsp baking soda
  1 C sugar
  1½ tsp cinnamon
  1 tsp nutmeg
  1 tsp ground ginger
  Optional: raisins, sliced apples, diced dried apricots, chopped carrot, chopped zucchini.

Preheat oven to 350°F (180°C). Generously grease a bundt or tube pan. Mix all ingredients together until smooth, adding 2 cups of optional ingredients to batter. Bake one hour. Remove from pan and cool on rack. Serve at room temperature.

Lady Fingers

Leavening agent: eggs

This particular recipe interested me because my grandmother used to buy lady fingers for a favorite family dessert called "Ice Box Cake." Over the years lady fingers have become difficult to find, so the dessert has been only a mouth-watering memory. I give you this recipe from the 1887 edition of *The White House Cookbook*, with the recipe for Ice Box Cake following on page 48.

  9 tbsp fine white sugar
  9 eggs
  9 tbsp sifted flour

Put sugar into a bowl and put the bowl into hot water to heat the sugar; when the sugar is thoroughly heated, break eggs into the bowl and beat them quickly until they become a little warm and rather thick; then take the bowl from the water and continue beating until it is nearly or quite cold; now stir in lightly sifted flour; then with a paper funnel, or something of the kind, lay this mixture out upon *papers, in biscuits three inches long and half an inch thick, in the form of fingers; sift sugar over the biscuits and bake them upon tins to a light brown; when they are done and cold, remove them from the papers, by wetting them on the back; dry them and they are ready for use. They are often used in making Charlotte Russe.

parchment paper

Ice Box Cake

This was a family favorite when I was a little girl. I'm not sure if German sweet chocolate is easy to find anymore, but bittersweet or dark chocolate would substitute nicely.

1½ dozen lady fingers (page 47)
5 bars German sweet chocolate
2 tbsp boiling water
4 eggs, separated

In the top of a double boiler dissolve chocolate in the 2 tablespoons of boiling water. Add the unbeaten yolks of eggs one by one, beating all the time. Then add whites beaten stiff. Line a small bread tin with parchment paper. Put in a layer of lady fingers, then a layer of chocolate mixture, and so on until the pan is filled. Let stand overnight in refrigerator. Slice and serve with whipped cream.

Loaf Cake

Leavening agents: emptings

From *The American Frugal Housewife*. I'm assuming "sweet emptings" mean they are fresh and haven't had time to sour.

2 pounds of flour (4 C)
½ pound sugar (1 C)
¼ pound butter (½ C)
2 eggs
1 gill of sweet emptings (½ C)
½ ounce cinnamon or cloves (1 tbsp)
large spoonful of lemon-brandy or rose-water

If it is not about as thin as good white bread dough, add a little milk. A common sized loaf is made by these proportions. Bake about ¾ of an hour.

Molasses Gingerbread

Leavening agents: pearlash and molasses

From Amelia Simmons's 1796 *American Cookery*.

1 tsp cinnamon
2 tsp ginger
pinch of coriander or allspice
1 tsp pearlash
4 C flour
1 C molasses
3 tbsp butter

Combine spices and flour; set aside. Mix pearlash and water; set aside. Blend molasses and butter, add water and pearlash, add flour and spices. Dough will be thick, roll out and cut to size with a cookie cutter or top of a cup. Bake 15 minutes at 375°F (165°C).

Short Cake

Leavening agents: pearlash, sour milk or buttermilk

From *The American Frugal Housewife*. Few measurements are given for the ingredients, only instructions. I'm guessing it is assumed that the baker has enough experience to achieve the desired dough consistency for success.

Sour milk or buttermilk
a bit of shortening or
3 tbsp cream
flour
1 tsp strong dissolved pearlash

"If you have sour milk, or butter-milk, it is well to make it into short cakes for tea. Rub in a very small bit of shortening, or three table-spoonfuls of cream with the flour; put in a tea-spoonful of strong dissolved pearlash into your sour milk, and mix your cake pretty stiff, to bake in the *spider on a few embers."

Spider - a cast iron skillet or pan with legs for cooking over campfire coals.

Sourdough Carob Chip Cake

Leavening agents: baking soda and sourdough starter

Another of my own recipes. Of course, chocolate chips may be substituted for carob chips.

½ C organic palm shortening
¾ C raw sugar
1 egg
½ C milk
1 C sourdough starter
1 C unbleached white flour
2 tsp baking soda
½ tsp salt
1 pkg unsweetened carob chips (about 2 C)

Cream shortening and sugar. Mix in egg, milk, and sourdough starter. Sift dry ingredients together and add to creamed mixture, stirring well. Fold in carob chips and pour into greased and floured Bundt pan. Bake at 350°F (180°C) for 40 minutes or until toothpick comes out clean.

Sponge Drops

Leavening agents: saleratus and cream of tartar

From the 1887 *The White House Cookbook*.

3 eggs
1 teacup of sugar (scant ¾ C)
1 heaping coffeecup of flour (1 C)
1 tsp cream of tartar
½ tsp saleratus

Beat to a froth the eggs and sugar; stir into this flour, in which cream of tartar and saleratus are thoroughly mixed. Flavor with lemon. Butter tin sheets with *washed butter and drop in teaspoonfuls about three inches apart. Bake instantly in a very quick oven (400-425°F/200-220°C). Watch closely as they will burn easily. Serve with ice cream.

Washed butter has been worked in cold water with a butter paddle to remove any remaining buttermilk. If not washed out, the buttermilk will begin to sour and give the butter a stronger, cultured butter flavor.

Tomato Juice Crumb Cake

Leavening agents: baking soda and tomato juice

Is tomato a fruit or a vegetable? I'll leave the answer up to you.

2 C sifted flour
⅔ C butter
1 tsp baking soda
1 tsp cinnamon
1 C raisins
1 C sugar
¼ tsp salt
1½ C tomato juice
¼ tsp cloves
1 egg
1 C currants

Mix together the flour and sugar, then add butter and rub this into mixture until in fine crumbs. Take out ¼ cup of these crumbs and reserve for top of cake. Add soda, cloves, and cinnamon to tomato juice and add to remaining crumbs. Beat egg well and add along with currants. Spread in a well-greased pan and sprinkle remaining crumbs on top. Bake in 350°F (180°C) oven for 40 to 50 minutes.

Tomato Juice Loaf Cake

Leavening agents: baking soda, tomato juice, and brown sugar

Another tomato based cake, equally delicious.

2 C tomato juice
1 C light brown sugar
6 tbsp softened butter
2 eggs
2 C flour
1 tsp baking soda
1 tsp cinnamon
1 tsp salt

Preheat the oven to 350°F (180°C). Grease and flour a loaf pan. Cream brown sugar and butter until light and fluffy. Beat in eggs one at a time, then mix in the tomato juice. Sift together the flour, baking soda, cinnamon, and salt in a bowl. Add the dry ingredients to the tomato-butter mixture and mix to combine. Pour into the prepared pan and bake until a toothpick inserted in the center comes out clean, about 45 to 50 minutes. Let cool slightly, then remove from the pan and transfer to a rack to cool completely before glazing.

Glaze
2 tbsp tomato juice
1 C confectioners' sugar

Mix and drizzle over cooled cake.

Vegan Chocolate Cake

Leavening agents: baking soda, cocoa powder, brown sugar, and vinegar

An ubiquitous internet recipe styled after "Wacky Cake" on page 52.

2¼ C flour
½ C cocoa powder (natural)
1 C sugar
½ C brown sugar
1 tsp baking soda
½ tsp salt
1 C water
½ C melted vegetable shortening
1 tsp vanilla
1 tbsp vinegar

Preheat oven to 350°F (180°C). Grease and flour a 9-inch bundt pan. Sift together flour and cocoa powder, then mix in the sugars, baking soda and salt.

Mix together the water, melted shortening, vanilla, and vinegar, then add to dry ingredients, mixing quickly. Pour into pan and bake for 45 to 50 minutes or until toothpick comes out clean. Allow to cool in pan for 10 minutes, then turn out onto a wire rack. Frost or glaze as desired.

Wacky Cake

Leavening agents: baking soda, cocoa powder, and vinegar

A well-known Depression Era cake, invented when dairy products were scarce.

> 1½ C all-purpose flour
> 1 C sugar
> ¼ C cocoa powder
> ½ tsp salt
> 1 tsp baking soda
> 1 tsp vanilla
> 1 tbsp vinegar
> ⅓ C melted shortening or vegetable oil
> 1 C cold water

Preheat oven to 350°F (180°C). Grease and flour an 8x8-inch baking pan. Measure dry ingredients into the baking pan, mix well. Make three holes in the flour mixture. Pour the vinegar into the first hole; the vanilla into the second hole, and the melted shortening or oil into the third. Pour water over all and mix thoroughly with a fork. Bake 35 to 40 minutes. May be served warm or cooled to frost.

Cookies

Crisp Cookies

Leavening agents: baking soda and cream of tartar

"Very Nice," says *The White House Cookbook*.

> 1 C butter
> 2 C sugar
> 3 eggs, well beaten
> 1 tsp soda
> 2 tsp cream of tartar
> 1 spoonful of milk
> 1 tsp of nutmeg
> 1 tsp of cinnamon
> flour, enough to make a soft dough just stiff enough to roll out

Try a pint (2 cups) of sifted flour to begin with, working it in gradually. Spread a little sweet milk over each and sprinkle with sugar. Bake to a light brown in a quick oven (375-400°F/190-200°C).

German Christmas Cookies

Leavening agent: hartshorn (baker's ammonia)

A very old German recipe.

> 1 C sugar
> ¼ tsp salt
> ½ C plus 2 tbsp butter
> 1 egg
> ½ C milk
> 1½ tsp hartshorn
> ¼ C boiling water
> 1 tsp vanilla
> 8 C flour, or enough to stiffen dough
> ½ oz anise seeds (1 tbsp)

Mix sugar, salt, shortening, eggs, and milk. In a separate bowl, dissolve the hartshorn in the boiling water. Make sure it is completely dissolved. Add vanilla and anise seeds to the sugar mixture, then add hartshorn mixture. Add enough flour to stiffen and not be sticky. Roll out dough on floured surface, and cut with cookie cutters. Bake immediately after mixing in a moderate oven (325-350°F/165-180°C) for 10 to 15 minutes. Makes about 100 cookies.

Gramma Wilson's Ginger Cookies

Leavening agents: baking soda and molasses

A childhood favorite with a glass of cold milk.

> ¾ C butter, melted & cooled
> 1 C sugar
> ¼ C molasses
> 1 egg
> 2 tsp baking soda
> ½ tsp salt
> 2 C flour
> ½ tsp cloves
> ½ tsp ginger
> 1 tsp cinnamon
> granulated sugar in a small bowl

Mix well and chill thoroughly. Form into 1-inch balls and roll in granulated sugar. Bake on greased cookie sheet at 375°F (190°C) for 8 to 10 minutes. Do not overbake. Makes 4 dozen.

Philadelphia Jumbles

Leavening agent: eggs

Another 1887 recipe from *The White House Cookbook.*

2 C sugar
1 C butter
8 eggs beaten light
essence of bitter almond or rose to taste
enough flour to enable you to roll them out

Stir the sugar and butter to a light cream, then add the well-whipped eggs, the flavoring and flour; mix well together, roll out in powdered sugar in a sheet a quarter of an inch thick; cut into rings with a *jagging-iron and bake in a quick oven (375-400°F/190-200°C) on buttered tins.

*Jagging-iron is similar to a ravioli crimping and cutting wheel.

Springerle

Leavening agent: hartshorn (baker's ammonia)

A traditional German Christmas cookie pressed with cookie molds or embossed rolling pins.

½ tsp hartshorn
1 tbsp milk
6 large eggs, room temperature
6 C powdered sugar
½ C softened unsalted butter
½ tsp salt
1½ tsp anise oil
8 C cake flour

Dissolve hartshorn in milk and set aside for about an hour. Sift powdered sugar into one bowl, sift flour into another. Beat eggs well (15 minutes) until thick. Slowly beat in the powdered sugar, then the softened butter. Beat in the dissolved hartshorn, salt, and anise oil. Add the flour slowly. If using a mixer, you will need to finish adding the flour by hand. Knead dough. It will be stiff but shouldn't be too sticky (add more flour if needed.) Divide into fourths, cover, and let rest for 30 minutes.

Roll out one of the fourths to ¼- to ⅜-inch thick. Use a lightly floured springerle rolling pin to imprint the dough (or use molds). Cut the cookies apart and allow to sit for 12 to 24 hours before baking. This dries the cookie so that the imprint remains during baking. High humidity requires the longer drying time. Bake at 275°F (140°C) for 15 to 20 minutes or until lightly browned on the bottom. Cool and store in airtight containers.

Swedish Christmas Cookies

Leavening agents: baking soda and sour milk

3 C flour
1 tsp salt
1 tsp baking soda
1¼ C sugar
⅔ C soft butter
2 tbsp sour milk
2 eggs, beaten
1 tsp almond extract
½ tsp vanilla
pinch cinnamon
⅓ C finely chopped almonds

Sift dry ingredients into mixing bowl. Blend in butter, eggs, sour milk, cinnamon, and vanilla. Mix well. Divide dough and roll into 2-inch thick logs. Rolls logs in chopped nuts and cut into ¼-inch slices. Bake at 325°F (165°C) until nicely browned.

White Ginger Biscuits

Leavening agents: baking soda and sour cream

The next three cookie recipes are from *The White House Cookbook*, published in 1887. For this one there isn't much for instructions, although the recipe mentions that sour milk may be substituted for the sour cream. I think a little salt would help the flavor.

1 C butter
2 C sugar
1 C sour cream
3 eggs
1 tsp soda dissolved in 1 tbsp warm water
1 tbsp ginger
1 tsp ground cinnamon
5 C of sifted flour, or enough to roll out soft
Optional: grated rind and juice of an orange

Cut out rather thick like biscuits; brush over the tops, while hot, with the white of an egg, or sprinkle with sugar while hot. The grated rind and the juice of an orange add much to the flavor of ginger cake.

White House Ginger Cookies
Leavening agents: baking soda, molasses, and vinegar

1 C sugar
1 C molasses
1 C butter
1 egg
1 tbsp vinegar
1 tbsp ginger
1 tsp soda dissolved in boiling water

Mix like cooky [sic] dough, rather soft.

White House Ginger Snaps
Leavening agents: baking soda, molasses, and brown sugar

1 C brown sugar
2 C molasses
1 large C butter
2 tsp soda
2 tsp ginger
3 pints flour to commence with (6 C)

Rub shortening and sugar together into the flour; add more flour as necessary to roll very smooth, very thin, and bake in a quick oven (375-400°F/190-200°C). The dough can be kept for days by putting it in the flour barrel under the flour, and bake a few at a time. The more flour that can be worked in and the smoother they can be rolled, the better and more brittle they will be. Should be rolled out to wafer-like thinness. Bake quickly without burning. They should become perfectly cold before putting aside.

Crackers

Butter Crackers

Leavening agent: baking soda

The instructions for this one gave me a chuckle. It's from *Common Sense in the Household: A Manual of Practical Housewifery*.

1 quart flour (4 C)
3 tbsp butter
½ tsp soda, dissolved in hot water
1 saltspoonful salt (¼ tsp)
2 cups *sweet milk

Rub butter into the flour, or what is better, cut it up with a knife or chopper as you do in pastry. Add the salt, milk, and soda, mixing well. Work into a ball, lay upon a floured board, and beat with a rolling-pin half an hour, turning and shifting the mass often. Roll into an even sheet, a quarter of an inch thick, or less, prick deeply with a fork, and bake hard in a moderate oven (325-350°F/165-180°C). Hang them up in a muslin bag in the kitchen for two days to dry.

Sweet milk - fresh milk, i.e. not soured.

Soda Crackers

Leavening agents: baking soda and cream of tartar

1 C flour
1 C lard
1 tsp salt
1 tsp baking soda
2 tsp cream of tartar
1½ C cold water

Mix flour, salt, and cream of tartar, then rub in shortening. Dissolve soda in cold water. Mix all ingredients. Roll out and bake in a quick oven (375-400°F/190-200°C).

Scottish Oat Crackers

Leavening agent: baking soda

1 C unbleached flour
1 C instant oatmeal
½ tsp salt
¼ tsp baking soda
¼ C butter melted in
½ C boiling water

Preheat oven to 325°F (170°C). Mix dry ingredients, then add butter melted in water. Knead in the bowl enough to mix, turn out onto floured board, and continue kneading until smooth. Roll thin, cut into squares, and prick with a fork. Bake on parchment paper for 10 to 15 minutes until crisp and brown. Cool and store in an airtight container.

Sour Milk Soda Crackers

Leavening agents: baking soda and sour milk

Sour milk
1 tsp butter, softened
½ tsp baking soda
1 tsp lard
3 C flour
coarse salt

Dissolve soda in a bit of sour milk and mix into the flour, enough to make a very stiff dough. Knead well working in butter and lard, and roll out very thin. Cut, shaping the crackers as you wish, sprinkle with coarse salt, and prick them in patterns with a fork. Bake in a moderate oven (350-375°F/180-190°C) until they are crisp (20 to 30 minutes).

Swedish Christmas Crackers

Leavening agent: hartshorn (baker's ammonia)

½ C scalded milk
¼ C cold milk
⅓ oz baker's ammonia
½ C lard
1½ C sugar
2 eggs, beaten
2 tsp lemon extract
3 to 4 C unbleached flour

Pour scalded milk over baker's ammonia in a small bowl. Set aside to cool. Cream lard and sugar in a mixing bowl, beat in eggs, lemon extract, cold milk, and 2 cups flour. Stir in the cooled baker's ammonia solution. Add another cup of flour to make a stiff batter. Continue adding flour ½ cup at a time until the dough is firm enough to roll out.

On a floured surface, roll the dough into a rectangle about 10 by 23 inches and ¼-inch thick. Cut into 2½-inch squares with a floured knife; place on baking sheets so they are not touching. Prick with a fork. Bake at 350°F (180°C) until golden brown, about 10 to 15 minutes. Remove from pans and cool on a baking rack. Makes about 36 crackers.

Swedish Thin Bread

Leavening agents: baking soda and sour cream

1 C sugar
2 C sour cream
2 C rye flour
1 tsp baking soda
2 C white flour
1 pinch salt

Mix sugar and sour cream. Mix dry ingredients, then combine with sugar mixture. Roll thinly on a floured board and cut into squares. Sprinkle with more salt. Bake at 350°F (180°C) until light brown, about 10 to 15 minutes.

Dumplings

Buttermilk Dumplings

Leavening agents: baking soda and buttermilk

A classic recipe..

2 C unbleached flour
1 tsp salt
1 tsp baking soda
¾ C buttermilk

Have your stew or broth simmering. Mix dry ingredients, then stir in buttermilk with a fork. Drop onto simmering liquid. Simmer on medium-low heat for 10 minutes or until dough is no longer glossy. Cover, reduce heat to low, and simmer another 10 minutes.

Muffins

"Coffee Cakes"

Leavening agents: baking soda and coffee

This was one of my experimental "no baking powder" recipes. The rise was impressive.

    1¾ C flour
    ½ C sugar
    ¼ C softened butter
    1 egg
    1 tsp baking soda
    ½ tsp salt
    1 tsp cinnamon
    ⅔ C strong regular coffee

Cream sugar and butter, add egg and mix well. Add dry ingredients and coffee, stirring enough to moisten. Bake in greased muffin tins for 12 minutes at 425°F (220°C). Makes one dozen.

Sourdough Zucchini Muffins

Leavening agents: baking soda and sourdough starter

From *5 Acres & A Dream The Blog: Q: Zucchini? A: Muffins.*

    2 C grated zucchini
    2 C unbleached white flour
    1 C sourdough starter (whole wheat)
    ½ C coconut oil or melted butter
    ½ C sugar
    1 egg
    ½ tbsp baking soda
    1 tsp salt
    ½ tsp nutmeg
    1 C milk

Blend all ingredients and mix well. Spoon into a greased or papered muffin pan and bake at 425°F (220°C) for about 25 to 30 minutes. Makes a dozen and a half.

Pancakes

Flat-jacks

Leavening agents: pearlash and sour beer

From *The American Frugal Housewife*: "Flat-jacks, or fritters, do not differ from pancakes, on in being mixed after. The same ingredients are used in about the same quantities; only most people prefer to have no sweetening put in them, because they generally have butter, sugar, and nutmeg, put on them, after they are done. Excepting for company, the nutmeg can be well dispensed with. They are not to be boiled in fat, like pancakes; the *spider or griddle should be well greased, and the cakes poured on as large as you want them, when it is quite hot, when if gets brown on one side, to be turned over upon other. Fritters are better to be baked quite thin. Either flour, Indian, or rye, is good.

Sour beer, with a spoonful of pearlash, is good for both pancakes and fritters."

½ pint milk (1 C)
1 or 2 eggs
1 tsp pearlash dissolved in
†sour beer
flour, ‡Indian, or rye

Spider - skillet or frying pan with legs for cooking over campfire coals.
†Sour beer - like all fermented things, the product continues to grow increasingly sour (acidic) with age. Combined with pearlash, this probably gave the flat-jacks a good rise. Any remaining alcohol would evaporate out during cooking.
‡Indian - corn meal

Sourdough Blueberry Pancakes

Leavening agents: baking soda and sourdough starter

2 C whole wheat sourdough starter
2 eggs
½ tsp salt
1 tsp baking soda
2 tbsp bacon grease
¼ C unbleached flour
¼ C milk
1 C fresh or thawed blueberries

Mix and cook like ordinary pancakes. Serve hot with butter and maple syrup.

Pastry

Cream Puffs

Leavening agent: eggs

Another very old recipe. This one came from my great grandmother.

For the puffs:
- 1 C boiling water
- ½ C butter
- 4 eggs
- 1 C flour
- ¼ tsp salt

Place water and butter in saucepan on high heat. When it comes to a boil, add flour and salt and stir until the dough pulls away from the side of the pan and forms a ball. Add eggs one at a time, beating with a fork until smooth and fluffy. Drop onto greased baking sheet and bake at 425°F (220°C) for 15 minutes, then 30 minutes at 325°F (165°C). Let set in oven until cool.

For the cream filling:
- 1 pint milk (2 C)
- ¼ C sugar
- 2 heaping tbsp flour
- 2 eggs
- salt and vanilla

Mix and cook over double boiler until thick and creamy.

Slice the puffs and pour filling over the bottom half. Replace the other half and top with your favorite fruit, sauce, or whipped cream. My grandmother served hers with chocolate sauce.

Miscellaneous

Homemade Baking Powder

- 1 part baking soda
- 2 parts cream of tartar
- 1 part corn starch or arrowroot powder

Mix and store in an airtight container.

Appendices

Chart of Baking Powder Substitutes

There are no hard and fast rules about substitutions for baking powder. The following are the most common recommendations found in various sources.

To Replace 1 Teaspoon of Baking Powder Use		
Ingredient	**Amount**	**Baking Soda**
Baker's Ammonia	1 tsp	none
Brown Sugar	⅓ C	¼ tsp
Buttermilk	½ C	½ tsp
Citric Acid	¼ tsp	1 tsp
Cocoa Powder (natural)	¼ C	¼ tsp
Coffee (strong, regular)	⅓ C	½ tsp
Cream of Tartar	½ tsp	¼ tsp
Fruit or Tomato Juice	1 C	½ tsp
Fruit or Tomato Sauce	1 C	½ tsp
Golden Syrup	⅜ C	¼ tsp
Honey	¼ C	¼ tsp
Kefir	½ C	½ tsp
Lemon Juice	½ tsp	¼ tsp
Maple Syrup	¼ C	¼ tsp
Molasses	¼ C	¼ tsp
Pickle Juice	½ tsp	¼ tsp
Sour Cream	½ C	½ tsp
Sour Milk	½ C	½ tsp
Sourdough Starter	1 C	1 tsp
Treacle	¼ C	¼ tsp
Vinegar	½ tsp	¼ tsp
Whey (acidic)	½ C	½ tsp
Yogurt (plain)	½ C	½ tsp

Typically recipes call for 1 teaspoon of baking powder per cup of flour, more if the recipe is richer in eggs and fats, or contains nuts, fruits, etc. Heavier ingredients require more leavening power.

When substituting ingredients for baking powder, other adjustments in the recipe may need to be made. For example, when using liquids such as sour dairy, honey, or molasses, remember to decrease the liquids called for in the recipe. If using sweeteners such as honey or molasses, sugar will need to be decreased.

The pH of Various Foods

pH - potential of Hydrogen. A scale indicating the activity of hydrogen ions in a solution. Ranges from 0 (extremely acidic) to 14 (extremely alkaline or basic). 7 is neutral.

For the science minded or those who simply want to experiment with recipes on their own, here is a reference chart of the pH of possible foods that might be used.

The basic science behind this is:

$$acid + carbonate \rightarrow salt + water + carbon\ dioxide$$

In this case the carbonate is the base, and carbon dioxide creates the bubbles that cause the product to rise. While our carbonates are somewhat limited, the acids are numerous and fun to experiment with. Actual values vary according to source, but these are the most common values that I found.

The Bases (all carbonates)	
Baking soda (sodium bicarbonate)	8.4
Baker's ammonia (ammonium carbonate)	9.0
Calcium carbonate (from eggshell)	9.4
Carbonate of soda (sodium carbonate)	11.6
Pearlash (potassium bicarbonate)	8.2
Potash (potassium carbonate)	11.5

The Acids (fruits are fresh unless otherwise noted)			
Apples	3.3 - 3.9	Brown sugar, dark	5.8 - 6.7
Apple juice	3.35 - 4.0	Brown sugar, light	5.8 - 6.5
Applesauce	3.1 - 3.6	Buttermilk	4.4 - 4.8
Apricots	3.3 - 4.8	Cherries	3.2 - 4.5
Bananas	4.5 - 5.2	Cider	2.9 - 3.3
Beer	4.0 - 5.0	Citric acid	2.2
Blackberries	3.9 - 4.5	Coffee, black	4.7 - 5.2
Blueberries	3.1 - 3.4	Cranberry juice	2.3 - 2.5

Cream of Tartar	4.85	Pickles, sour	3.0 - 3.4
Dates	4.1 - 4.8	Pineapple	3.2 - 4.0
Figs	5.0 - 6.0	Pineapple, canned	3.4 - 4.1
Gooseberries	2.8 - 3.1	Pineapple juice, canned	3.3 - 3.6
Grapefruit	3.0 - 3.7	Plums	2.8 - 3.0
Grapes	3.5 - 4.5	Pomegranate	2.9 - 3.2
Grape juice	2.9 - 3.5	Prune juice	3.9 - 4.0
Kefir	4.5	Pumpkin	4.8 - 5.2
Lemons	2.2 - 2.4	Raspberries	3.2 - 3.6
Lemon juice	2.0 - 2.6	Rhubarb	3.1 - 3.2
Limes	1.8 - 2.0	Sauerkraut	3.4 - 3.6
Lime juice	2.0 - 2.4	Sour cream	4.5
Loganberries	2.7 - 3.5	Strawberries	3.0 - 3.9
Mangoes	3.4 - 4.8	Tea, black	5.0 - 6.0
Maple syrup	4.6 - 5.5	Tea, green	6.0 - 7.0
Molasses	4.9 - 5.4	Tomatoes	4.3 - 4.9
Muscadines	3.2 - 3.4	Tomatoes, juice	4.1 - 4.6
Nectarines	3.9 - 4.2	Tomatoes, puree	4.3 - 4.5
Oranges	3.0 - 4.0	Vegetable juice	3.9 - 4.3
Orange juice	3.3 - 4.2	Vinegar, white	2.4 - 3.4
Papaya	2 - 6.0	Vinegar, cider	3.1
Peaches	3.4 - 4.1	Watermelon	5.2 - 5.6
Pears	3.6 - 4.0	Wines	2.8 - 3.8
Persimmons	4.4 - 4.7	Yogurt, plain	4.2 - 4.5
Pickles, dill	3.2 - 3.6		

Resources

The following are not an endorsement, but for your convenience. Hopefully the sites will remain up and running for a very long time.

For help with historical measurements and cookery terms
"An 18th Century Cooking Glossary," *Paula Walton's 18th Century Home Journal*, https://paulawalton.wordpress.com/2010/10/27/an-eighteenth-century-cooking-glossary/
"Breakfast Cups and Tea Cups," *Lois Elsden*
https://loiselden.com/2015/08/16/breakfast-cups-and-tea-cups/
MSU's online glossary of historical cooking terms
http://digital.lib.msu.edu/projects/cookbooks/html/glossary.html
MSU's online museum of historical kitchen utensils and equipment
http://digital.lib.msu.edu/projects/cookbooks/html/museum.html
"Oven Temperatures," *Hints and Things*, includes degrees Fahrenheit and Celsius, gas marks, and historical descriptions.
http://www.hintsandthings.co.uk/kitchen/oventemp.htm
"Terms, Weights, Measures," *Vintage Recipes*
http://www.vintagerecipes.net/glossary.php

How to make potash
"A Primitive Alkali: Potash," *Caveman Chemistry*
http://cavemanchemistry.com/oldcave/projects/potash/
(scroll to the bottom of the page)

Where to buy buttermilk starter
New England Cheesemaking Supply Company
http://www.cheesemaking.com/shop/buttermilk-ds-culture-5-pack.html

Where to buy baker's ammonia
The Great American Spice Company
https://www.americanspice.com/baking-ammonia-ammonium-carbonate-bulk-16-oz/
Science Company
http://www.sciencecompany.com/Ammonium-Carbonate-Bakers-Ammonia-Food-Grade-8-oz-P16462.aspx
Olde Town Spice Shoppe
http://www.oldtownspices.com/p-394-bakers-ammonia-hartshorn.aspx

Where to buy other historical leaveners
    Pearlash (potassium carbonate)
        Sierra Chemical Co., http://www.sierrachemicalcompany.com/
        index.php?page=shop.product_details&category_id=6&product_id=
        150&option=com_virtuemart
    Saleratus (potassium bicarbonate)
        Nuts.com, https://nuts.com/cookingbaking/leavenerthickener/
        potassium-bicarbonate.html
    Carbonate of Soda (sodium carbonate)
        Sierra Chemical Co., http://www.sierrachemicalcompany.com/
        index.php?page=shop.product_details&flypage=flypage.tpl&product
        _id=159&category_id=6&keyword=sodium+carbonate&option=com
        _virtuemart&Itemid=2

For More Historical Recipes
    The American Frugal Housewife by Lydia Child (online edition)
        https://archive.org/details/americanfrugalhooochil
    Mrs. Beeton's Book of Household Management (online edition)
        http://www.mrsbeeton.com/index.html
    History Cookbook (from prehistoric to modern recipes)
        http://cookit.e2bn.org/historycookbook/
    MSU online historic cookbook collection from *Feeding America:*
        The Historic American Cookbook Project (PDFs)
        http://digital.lib.msu.edu/projects/cookbooks/html/browse.html
    The Practice Of Cookery by Mrs. Dalgairns, 1840 (online edition)
        http://www.electricscotland.com/food/cookery/index.htm
    Vintage Recipes (index of collections)
        http://www.vintagerecipes.net/books/

Glossary

Acid - A substance with a pH below 7. Acidic foods are usually sour to taste.

Akaun (or Kaun) - Cooking potash used in Nigerian cuisine.

Albumin - The protein found in egg whites.

Alkali (also called a base) - A substance with a pH above 7. In cooking, an alkali will be slippery to touch and slightly bitter to taste.

Baked goods - Broad category of foods baked in an oven such as cookies, cakes, pastries, etc.

Baker's ammonia - Ammonium carbonate, $(NH_4)_2CO_3$. A heat-activated leavening agent once made from the antlers of male deer (hartshorn). The ammonia dissipates during baking, giving the product a distinctive light texture. Favored for a number of German cookie recipes.

Baking powder - A convenient leavening agent for quick breads. Contains at least one acid and a base.

Baking soda - Sodium bicarbonate or bicarbonate of soda, $(NaHCO_3)$.

Barm - The yeasty foam which forms on top of beer, ale, or hard cider during the brewing process.

Base (also called an alkali) - A substance with a pH above 7. In cooking, a base will be slippery to touch and slightly bitter to taste.

Biological leavening - Leavening action caused by various forms of yeast which creates carbon dioxide bubbles which cause the product to rise. Used in products such as breads and rolls.

Breakfast-cup - Old-fashioned measurement which was larger than a "teacup." One large breakfast-cupful is roughly equivalent to 1.5 cups, a small breakfast cupful is approximately one cup.

Brisk oven (quick oven) - a hot oven of 375-400°F (190-200°C).

Buttermilk - a. *Traditional* - the liquid remaining after butter churning.

b. *Cultured* - milk into which a specific buttermilk culture has been introduced and allowed to work.

Caster (castor) sugar - A British grade of sugar called "superfine" in the U.S. It is finer than granulated sugar, but coarser than powdered sugar.

Chemical leavening - Leavening action caused by compounds which create carbon dioxide bubbles in the presence of moisture or heat.

Citric acid - ($C_6H_8O_7$). A weak naturally-occurring acid found in citrus fruits. It is also manufactured industrially.

Clabber (clabbered) - Separate(ed) into curds and whey.

Cracklings - Byproduct of rendering animal fat. Consists of the bits of unmelted fat and meat which are strained out and used as flavoring.

Cream of tartar - Potassium bitartrate, ($KC_4H_5O_6$). An acidic chemical obtained from the fermentation of grapes. Found in tartrate baking powders.

Double-acting baking powders - Contain a base (baking soda) and two acids, one quick acting, the other with a slightly slower reaction time.

Dutch processing - Treating cocoa with an alkali to neutralize its pH. Makes a darker, mild-flavored chocolate with reduced antioxidants. Being neutral, it is not a good chemical leavening agent.

Emptings (Emptyings, Emptins) - the yeasty dregs at the bottom of the beer or ale brewing barrel.

Gill - A one-half cup measurement.

Hardwood - Wood from dicot angiosperm trees, i.e. flowering trees which have two embryonic leaves. In general, they have broad leaves, produce a fruit or nut, and go dormant in the winter.

Hartshorn - Historically, the ground-up antlers of a male deer (hart). Synthetically produced as ammonium carbonate (baker's ammonia).

Hominy - Corn which has been soaked in an alkali solution to remove the germ and hulls.

Indian - Indian meal or corn meal.

Kaun (or Akaun) - Cooking potash used in Nigerian cuisine.

Kosher for Passover baking powder - Contains potato starch rather than corn starch.

Lactobacillus - Naturally occurring bacteria found in milk before it has been pasteurized. It feeds on the sugars in the milk (lactose) converting them to lactic acid. It is the lactic acid that eventually gives milk the sour smell and taste.

Leaven, Leavening - *Noun* - A substance which produces carbon dioxide bubbles through fermentation, causing bread and baked goods to rise. *Verb* - To make light, to cause to rise.

Lihiya - A food grade lye water made and sold in the Philippines.

Lutefisk - Scandinavian dish in which dried fish is brined in lye water.

Lye - can refer to sodium hydroxide (caustic soda) or potassium hydroxide (caustic potash).

Lye water - lye diluted with water. Used in many cultures for cooking.

Masa - Nixtamalized corn meal.

Moderate oven - 325-350°F (160-180°C).

Molasses - Dark, sweet, liquid byproduct of the sugar refining process.

Mordant - A substance which assists the bonding of color to fabric in the dyeing process.

Natural cocoa - Has not been Dutch processed.

Nixtamalization - Process of soaking grain (usually corn) in a highly alkaline solution to loosen the outer hull. The process increases both digestibility and nutrient content of the grain.

Pearlash - Potassium carbonate (K_2CO_3) refined from potash.

pH - Potential of Hydrogen. A scale indicating the activity of hydrogen ions in a solution. 0 is extremely acidic, 14 is extremely alkaline, and 7 is neutral.

Phosphate baking powders - Contain calcium phosphate or disodium pyrophosphate plus sodium bicarbonate.

Piki bread - Traditional Hopi bread made of blue corn meal and local plant ashes.

Potash - Potassium salts obtained through mining or manufacture.

Pottasche - German spelling for potash.

Quick bread - A bread made with a leavening agent that does not require time to rise (as with yeast) but permits immediate baking.

Quick oven - 375-400°F (190-200°C).

Room temperature - generally considered to be 68-72°F (20-22°C).

Saleratus - From the Latin for "aerated salt." Originally potassium bicarbonate ($KHCO_3$), later sodium bicarbonate ($NaHCO_3$).

Saltspoon - One-quarter teaspoon. Salt spoons once accompanied salt cellars, which were used in the days before salt shakers.

SAS baking powder - Contains sodium aluminum sulfate [$NaAl(SO_4)_2\cdot 12H_2O$] as its base. SAS is activated by heat rather than liquids.

Shelf life - The length of time a food item may be stored for maximum taste, nutrition, and potency.

Single-acting baking powders - Contain a base (baking soda) and one acid.

Slack oven - A very slow oven - 225-250°F (110-130°C).

Slow oven - 275-300°F (120-140°C).

Sour dairy - any sour dairy product: sour milk, sour cream, yogurt, kefir, etc.

Sour milk - Milk in which the naturally occurring lactobacillus has converted the lactose (milk sugar) into lactic acid, giving it a sour smell and taste.

Spider - A frying pan or skillet with legs. Used to cook over the hot coals of a fireplace or campfire.

Sweet milk - Fresh milk, not soured. This term is found in old recipes dating before the days of refrigeration.

Tartrate Baking Powder - Contains tartaric acid ($KC_4H_5O_6$), i.e. cream of tartar or potassium bitartrate plus sodium bicarbonate ($NaHCO_3$).

Teacupful - A scant three-quarter cup.

Treacle - Food grade molasses (term commonly used in the UK).

Very quick oven - 400-425°F (200-220°C).

Bibliography

"American Pot-Ash Cake," *The Scots Magazine*, December 1799, accessed January 12, 2016, http://worldturndupsidedown.blogspot.com/2014/09/american-potash-cake-or-long-island.html.

"Answers to Frequently Asked Questions about Kefir," *Dom's Kefir FAQ IN-site*, last modified June 26, 2015, accessed February 10, 2016, http://users.chariot.net.au/~dna/kefir-faq.html#kefiride.

Audet, Marye, "Why Duck Eggs Are Charming Chefs," *CulinaryOne*, last modified April 6, 2013, accessed March 26, 2016, http://www.culinaryone.com/why-duck-eggs-are-charming-chefs-in-2013/.

"Baking Powder," *Cooks Info*, accessed January 2, 2016, http://www.cooksinfo.com/baking-powder.

"Baking Powder," *Wikipedia*, last modified November, 27, 2015, accessed November 30, 2015, https://en.wikipedia.org/wiki/Baking_powder.

"Baking Powder and Baking Soda (Bicarbonate)," *Joy of Baking*, accessed December 1, 2015, http://www.joyofbaking.com/bakingsoda.html.

"Baking Powder Substitutions," *FitDay.com*, accessed December 1, 2015, http://www.fitday.com/fitness-articles/nutrition/healthy-eating/baking-powder-substitutions.html.

"Baking Soda," *Bon Appétit*, last modified August 10, 2008. accessed December 1, 2015, http://www.bonappetit.com/test-kitchen/cooking-tips/article/baking-soda.

"Bases - pH Values," *The Engineering ToolBox*, accessed February 10, 2016, http://www.engineeringtoolbox.com/bases-ph-d_402.html.

Beeton, Isabella, *Mrs. Beeton's Book of Household Management*, accessed February 13, 2016, http://www.mrsbeeton.com/index.html.

"Brown Sugar," *United Sugars Corporation*, accessed Febuary 10. 2016, http://unitedsugars.com/productsBrownSugar.html.

Chase, Alvin Wood, *Dr. Chase's third, last and complete receipt book and household physician*, Sydney: Malcolm & Grigg, 1887.

Child, Lydia, *The American Frugal Housewife, Dedicated To Those Who Are Not Ashamed of Economy*, 22nd edition, New York: Samuel S. & William Wood, 1838.

Choudhury, Ankana Dey, "Baking Powder Substitutes," *Buzzle*, last modified December 27, 2012, accessed November 30, 2015, http://www.buzzle.com/articles/baking-powder-substitute.html.

"Coenraad Johannes van Houten," *Wikipedia*, last modified March 3, 2015, accessed December 17, 2015, https://en.wikipedia.org/wiki/Coenraad_Johannes_van_Houten.

Dunn, Kevin, M., "Potash," *From Caveman To Chemist*, accessed December 10, 2015, http://cavemanchemistry.com/oldcave/projects/potash/.

"Dutch Process Chocolate," *Wikipedia*, last modified October 25, 2015, accessed December 1, 2015, https://en.wikipedia.org/wiki/Dutch_process_chocolate.

Edwards, W. P., editor, *The Science of Bakery Products*, 2007, accessed November 30, 2015, https://books.google.com/books?id=oCVPjKom SfkC&lpg=PP1&pg=PA73&hl=en#v=onepage&q&f=false.

"Eggs," *Joy of Baking*, accessed December 10, 2015, http://www.joyofbaking.com/eggs.html.

Elsden, Lois, "Breakfast Cups and Tea Cups," *Lois Elsden*, last modified August 16, 2015, accessed February 17, 2016, http://loiselden.com/2015/08/16/breakfast-cups-and-tea-cups/.

Fankhauser, David, B., "Making Buttermilk," *University of Cincinnati Clermont College*, last modified June 14 2007, accessed November 20, 2015, http://biology.clc.uc.edu/fankhauser/Cheese/BUTTERMILK.HTM.

"Food and Foodstuff - pH Values," *The Engineering ToolBox*, accessed Feburary 10. 2016, http://www.engineeringtoolbox.com/food-ph-d_403.html.

Gillette, Mrs. F.L. and Ziemann, Hugo, Steward of the White House, *The White House Cookbook: The Whole Comprising a Comprehensive Cyclopedia of Information for the Home*, 1887.

Gottleib, Marc, "Citric Acid and The Science of Meringue," *Culinart Kosher*, last modified June 11, 2012, accessed January 2, 2016, http://cooking.marc gottlieb.com/2012/06/citric-acid-and-the-science-of-meringue/.

Grierson, Alice Kirk, *An Army Wife's Cookbook*, N.P.: Western National Parks Association, 1972.

Green, Denzil, "Baking Powder," *Cook's Info*, accessed November, 28, 2015, http://www.cooksinfo.com/baking-powder.

Harland, Marion, *Common Sense in the Household: A Manual of Practical Housewifery*, Charles Scribner's Sons: New York, 1893.

Hess, Karen, transcriber, *Martha Washington's Booke of Cookery and Booke of Sweetmeats*, Columbia University Press: New York, 1995.

"How to Cream Butter," *Baking Library*, last modified July 21, 2010, accessed February 20, 2016, http://bakinglibrary.blogspot.com/2010/07/how-to-cream-butter.html.

"How to Make Substitute Baking Powder," *wikiHow*, accessed November 30, 2015, http://www.wikihow.com/Make-Substitute-Baking-Powder.

"Information on Hartshorn," *Goode Cookies from Gode Cookery*, accessed December 24, 2015, http://www.godecookery.com/cookies/infoba.html.

Kruger, Jake, "Eggshell (Calcium Carbonate) Leavening, Part 1," *The Homestead Laboratory*, last modified February 20, 2016, accessed February 25, 2016, http://homesteadlaboratory.blogspot.com/2016/02/eggshell-calcium-carbonate-leavening.html.

Kruger, Jake, "Eggshell (Calcium Carbonate) Leavening, Part 2," *The Homestead Laboratory*, last modified February 29, 2016, accessed March 26, 2016, http://homesteadlaboratory.blogspot.com/2016/02/eggshell-calcium-carbonate-leavening_29.html.

Lohman, Sarah, "The History Dish: Pearlash, The First Chemical Leavening," *Four Pounds Flour*, last modified May 23, 2012, accessed January 13, 2016, http://www.fourpoundsflour.com/the-history-dish-pearlash-the-first-chemical-leavening/.

Manthey, David, "A Comparison of Leavening Agents," 2002, accessed April 6, 2016, http://orbitals.com/self/leaven/.

McGavin, Jennifer, "Potash and Pearlash - German Baking Aid," German Baking Glossary, *About Food*, accessed January 21, 2015, http://germanfood.about.com/od/germanfoodglossary/g/Pearlash-German-Baking-Aid.htm.

McGee, Harold, "For Old-Fashioned Flavor, Bake the Baking Soda," *The New York Times*, last modified September 14, 2010, accessed February 13, 2016, http://www.nytimes.com/2010/09/15/dining/15curious.html?_r=0.

O'Connell, Dorian, "Duck Eggs vs Chicken Eggs in Baking," *101 Sweet Pastry*, last modified January 16, 2014, accessed March 26, 2016, http://101sweetpastry.com/duck-eggs-vs-chicken-eggs-in-baking/.

O'Dwyer, Edward J., "Oldest reference to a published Soda Bread recipe," *The Society for the Preservation of Irish Soda Bread*, last modified 2003, accessed January 20, 2016, http://www.sodabread.info/oldest-reference-to-soda-bread/.

Paynter, Henry, M., "The First Patent," accessed February 2, 2016, http://www.me.utexas.edu/~longoria/paynter/hmp/The_First_Patent.html.

Pavlik, Jeff, "An Experiment with Period & Non-Period Leaveners," *Colonial Baker*, accessed January 15, 2016, http://colonialbaker.net/leavening_experiment.html.

"pH of Foods and Food Products," *PickYourOwn.org*, accessed February 10, 2016, http://www.pickyourown.org/ph_of_foods.htm.

"Potash," *Wikipedia*, last modified February 2, 2016, accessed February 3, 2016, https://en.wikipedia.org/wiki/Potash.

"Pot-Ash-Cake," *The Domestic Encyclopaedia* Vol 3, Willich, A. F. M. editor, published 1802, online version accessed February 20, 2016, http://chestofbooks.com/reference/The-Domestic-Encyclopaedia-Vol3/Pot-Ash-Cake.html.

"Potassium Bitartrate," *Wikipedia*, last modified December 27, 2015, accessed January, 2, 2016, https://en.wikipedia.org/wiki/Potassium_bitartrate.

"Potassium Carbonate," *Wikipedia*, last modified June 19, 2016, accessed June 21, 2016, https://en.wikipedia.org/wiki/Potassium_carbonate.

"Quick Bread Primer," *King Arthur Flour*, accessed February 5, 2016, http://www.kingarthurflour.com/tips/quick-bread-primer.html.

"Saleratus," *Cook's Info*, accessed December 18. 2015, http://www.cooksinfo.com/saleratus.

"Saleratus," *Joe Pastry: Baking Techniques, History, & Science*, last modified Novenber 18, 2014, accessed January 30, 2016, http://joepastry.com/2014/saleratus/.

"Saleratus to Baking Soda," *Joe Pastry: Baking Techniques, History, & Science*, last modified March 21, 2011, accessed December 18, 2015, http://joepastry.com/2011/saleratus-to-soda/.

"Science: Acids, bases and salts: Reactions of acids: Carbonates," *BBC*, accessed January 23, 2016, http://www.bbc.co.uk/schools/gcsebitesize/science/add_aqa_pre_2011/ions/acidsbasesrev2.shtml.

Simmons, Amelia, *American Cookery*, N.p.:Hudson & Goodwin, 1796.

Slave Narratives: A Folk History of Slavery in the United States, Federal Writers Project of the Works Progress Administration, Washington, 1936-1941, accessed December 15, 2015, http://memory.loc.gov/mss/mesn/042/042.1.txt, http://www.fullbooks.com/Slave-Narratives-Arkansas-Narratives1.html, and http://www.faithfabric.com/lifehistories/georgia/18farming_preacher.htm.

"Sodium Carbonate," Wikipedia, last modified February 1, 2016, accessed February 13, 2016, https://en.wikipedia.org/wiki/Sodium_carbonate.

"Sodium Hydroxide," *Wikipedia*, last modified March 18, 2016, accessed April 1, 2016, https://en.wikipedia.org/wiki/Sodium_hydroxide.

"Sourdough," *Wikipedia*, last modified March 9, 2016, accessed April 5, 2016, https://en.wikipedia.org/wiki/Sourdough.

Stauffer, Clyde, E., *Functional Additives for Bakery Foods*, Dordrecht, Netherland: Kluwer Academic / Plenum Publishers, 1995, online edition accessed November 30, 2015, http://www.google.com/books?id=ckfdE5sRbqAC&lpg=PP1&pg=PA193#v=onepage&q=&f=false.

Tate, Leigh "Baking With Wood Ash?," *5 Acres & A Dream The Blog*, last modified January 23, 2016, accessed January 23, 2016, http://www.5acresandadream.com/2016/01/baking-with-wood-ash-part-1.html.

Walker, Barbara M., *The Little House Cookbook: Frontier Foods from Laura Ingalls Wilder's Classic Stories*, N.p.:Harper Collins Publishers, 1976.

Wasserman, Robin, "Uses of Potassium Hydroxide," *Livestrong*, last modified August 16, 2013, accessed April 1, 2016, http://www.livestrong.com/article/122647-uses-potassium-hydroxide/.

"Where does soda bread come from?," *Joe Pastry: Baking Techniques, History, & Science*, last modified March 15, 2011, accessed December 18, 2015, http://joepastry.com/2011/where-does-soda-bread-come-from/.

Wright, John D., *The Language of the Civil War*, N.p., Greenwood, 2001.

About the Author

Leigh Tate and her husband Dan homestead five acres in the foothills of the southern Appalachian Mountains. Their goals are simpler, sustainable, more self-reliant living, and a return to agrarian values. In addition to critter keeping, gardening, food preservation, cheese making, and woodstove cookery, Leigh loves to write about homesteading. She is the author of *5 Acres & A Dream The Book: The Challenges of Establishing a Self-Sufficient Homestead*, an eBook series entitled *The Little Series of Homestead How-Tos*, and *Critter Tales: What my homestead critters have taught me about themselves, their world, and how to be a part of it*. Her ongoing homestead adventures can be read at her blog, *5 Acres & A Dream The Blog*.

Also by Leigh Tate

5 Acres & A Dream The Book:
The Challenges of Establishing
a Self-Sufficient Homestead

When Leigh and Dan Tate bought an old farm house on five acres, their dream was a simpler life. Their goal was sustainable, self-reliant living. *5 Acres & A Dream The Book* shares how they set about to make their dream a reality and the challenges they have faced along the way: from defining their goals, finding property, and setting priorities, to obstacles and difficult times, to learning how to work smarter, not harder. She shares what they've learned about energy, water, and food self-sufficiency for themselves and their animals too. Included are copies of their homestead master plan, plus revisions, and a sampling of Leigh's homestead recipes. Paperback.

Visit http://kikobian.com/5acres.html for chapter titles and where to buy.

Critter Tales: What my homestead critters
have taught me about themselves, their
world, and how to be a part of it

Similar in style to *5 Acres and a Dream, Critter Tales* presents an entertaining but honest exploration of the challenges of sustainable critter keeping on a self-reliant homestead: suitable breeds, numbers, housing, fencing, growing one's own feed, health issues, mysterious disappearances and deaths, dealing with predators, critters that won't stay put, and how the animals themselves don't always agree with "the experts." Discusses the various philosophies of keeping livestock, and includes the author's careful research and real-life learning experiences with chickens, goats, llamas, dogs, guinea fowl, cats, pigs, and honeybees on the homestead. Paperback.

For more information visit http://kikobian.com/Critter_Tales.html.

How To Preserve Eggs

Leigh Tate

The Little Series of Homestead How-Tos
an eBook series

Most homesteading how-to books start at the beginning. They are written to equip the aspiring homesteader to get started in homesteading: how to garden, how to preserve food, how to get started with livestock, etc. This eBook series offers "next step" skills to further enhance the homesteader's self-reliance and sustainability.

Available formats: epub, mobi (Kindle), pdf, rtf, lrf, pdb, txt, and html.

How To Preserve Eggs:
freezing, pickling, dehydrating, larding, water glassing, & more
How To Make a Buck Rag:
& other good things to know about breeding your goats
How To Make an Herbal Salve:
an introduction to salves, creams, ointments, & more
How To Mix Feed Rations With The Pearson Square:
grains, protein, calcium, phosphorous, balance, & more
How To Garden For Goats:
gardening, foraging, small-scale grain and hay, & more
How-To Home Soil Tests:
10 DIY tests for texture, pH, drainage, earthworms & more
How To Make Mozzarella from Goats Milk:
plus what to do with all that whey including make ricotta
How To Bake Without Baking Powder:
modern and historical alternatives for light and tasty baked goods
How To Grow Ginger: how to grow, harvest, use, and perpetuate this
tropical spice in a non-tropical climate
How To Get Cream from Goats' Milk:
make your own butter, whipped cream, ice cream & more
How To Make Amish Whitewash:
make your own whitewash, paint, and wood stain
To Draw Blood from a Goat:
how to collect and send specimens to test for pregnancy, Johnes, CAE, CL, and more
To Compost With Chickens:
work smarter not harder for faster compost & happier chickens

For the latest titles visit http://kikobian.com/little_series.html.

Prepper's Livestock Handbook:
Lifesaving Strategies and Sustainable
Methods for Keeping Chickens, Rabbits,
Goats, Cows and Other Farm Animals

Livestock care from a preparedness point of view.

You will learn: which livestock is best suited to preparedness, options for shelter and fencing, how to establish and maintain good pasture, how to grow and store hay, strategies for feeding your farm animals without going to the feed store, options for breeding, birthing, veterinary care, and sustainable dairying. Also pitfalls to avoid and how to keep things manageable. If the grid ever fails, you will know how to preserve and store eggs, dairy foods, and meat without electricity. The *Preppers Livestock Handbook* focuses on simple, low-tech, off-grid methods for managing your land and your livestock. Covers cattle, goats, sheep, pigs, rabbits, and poultry (chickens, ducks, geese, turkeys, and guinea fowl). Available in paperback and eBook.

For more information and where to buy visit
http://kikobian.com/Preppers_Livestock.html

Index

A

acid
  carbonic, 19
  citric, 11
  in baking powder, 1
  kitchen, 5, 11
  tartaric, 4, 42
acidic
  ingredients, 3, 10, 15, 19, 27
  whey, 38
acidity, 5
aerated salt, 18
albumin, 30
ale, 11, 19, 28
alkali, 1, 3, 10, 15, 29
  food grade, 15
alkaline
  aftertaste, 17, 19, 43
  batteries, 26
  salts, 10
  substance, 1
alkalinization, 10
ammonia, 17
ammonium
  carbonate, 15, 17, 27
  hydroxide, 17
apple cider vinegar, 33
arrowroot powder, 2, 62
ash water, 21-27, 37, 40, 41
  how to make, 37
  recipes using, 37, 40
Asian noodles, 15, 21, 26, 28

B

baked soda, 28
baker's ammonia, 15, 17, 19, 64
  recipes using, 53, 54, 58
baking, 9, 15-18, 26, 32
  bread, 13
  experiments, 18, 19, 22-25
  pans, 32
  sourdough, 13

  temperatures, 3, 32
baking powder
  cocoa and, 10
  double-acting, 1, 4
  experiments with, 19
  homemade, 1, 62
  fast-acting, 1
  kinds of, 1
  kosher, 1
  phosphate, 1
  SAS, 1
  shelf life of, 2
  single-acting, 1
  slow-acting, 1
  starch in, 4
  substitutes for, 5, 15, 17
  tartrate, 1, 4
  testing potency, 2
baking soda
  as substitute, 4, 5, 11
  cocoa powder and, 10
  experiments with, 19
  heat activation, 3
  in baking powder, 1-3
  precursors of, 18, 19, 21
  sourdough and, 13
  substitutes for, 15
  uses, 3
  volcano reaction, 22
barm, 19, 28
batter, 1-3, 7, 13, 15, 30, 32
beer, 11, 28
  recipes using, 36, 61
bicarbonate of soda, 13, 18
bicarbonate salts, 21
biodiesel, 26
biscuits, experimental, 19, 22, 23
brown sugar, 11, 64
  recipes using, 51, 56
buffer, 1
buttermilk, 3, 5, 33, 64
  commercial, 8

(vinegar continued)
    recipes using, 51, 52, 56
    substituting, 33
    white, 22, 23, 33

W

washing soda, 28
whey, 11, 13, 33, 38
    acidic, 38
white
    flour, 13, 23, 37
    vinegar, 22, 23, 33
whole grain flour, 1, 37
wine, 4, 11
    recipe using, 43
wood ash, 18, 21-26
    recipes using, 37, 40

Y

yogurt, 5, 8, 33, 37
    recipes using, 38, 45
    substituting, 33
yeast
    airborne, 13
    baking (active dry), 13, 19, 28, 46
    brewing, 28
    natural, 13
    sourdough starter and, 14

Notes

Notes

Notes

Made in the USA
Monee, IL
28 September 2021